T0278314

UNIVERSITY OF MICHIGAN
BASKETBALL, 1960–1989
From Cazzie Russell to the NCAA Title

MIKE ROSENBAUM

THE
History
PRESS

Published by The History Press
Charleston, SC
www.historypress.com

First published 2024

Manufactured in the United States

ISBN 9781467155359

Library of Congress Control Number: 2023940685

CONTENTS

ACKNOWLEDGEMENTS

Thanks to Greg Kinney and the staff at the Bentley Historical Library for their help finding research materials and photos, as well as to the staff at the Ann Arbor Public Library.

This book is based primarily on interviews with U-M players and coaches. Several people helped me reach out to some of those subjects, most notably Tom Wywrot, Michigan basketball's sports information director.

Above all, thanks to the current and former players and coaches for so generously giving their time to talk about their Michigan basketball experiences, while asking nothing in return. Special thanks to the players and coaches who helped me connect with other interview subjects.

The subjects interviewed specifically for this book, in alphabetical order, are: Mike Boyd, Oliver Darden, Dan Fife, Bill Frieder, Gary Grant, Rickey Green, Steve Grote, Phil Hubbard, Mark Hughes, Ernest Johnson, Joe Johnson, Antoine Joubert, Tim McCormick, Terry Mills, Johnny Orr, George Pomey, Glen Rice, Les Rockymore, Campy Russell, Cazzie Russell, Jim Skala, Tom Staton, Dave Strack, Rudy Tomjanovich, Loy Vaught, Butch Wade and Perry Watson.

INTRODUCTION

This book begins in 1960. The University of Michigan basketball program does not. The author intends no disrespect to anyone who played, coached or supported U-M basketball from 1909 to 1960, but it's undeniable that Michigan basketball leveled up in the 1960s as Coach Dave Strack's teams, led by players such as Cazzie Russell and Bill Buntin, won three straight Big Ten championships and appeared in back-to-back Final Fours. Until that point, U-M had totaled five conference titles—four in a nine-year span in the 1920s—and one NCAA tournament appearance.

Another reason to begin in 1960 is that this book is based on new interviews with Wolverines players and coaches. Obviously, the farther back in time you go, the fewer people are available who can share their perspectives on Michigan basketball. When I interviewed Strack, for example, he was approaching his eighty-seventh birthday.

Interviewing players and coaches several decades after their active years leads to a fresh perspective on this era of U-M basketball. The interview subjects can speak more freely, with no concerns about offering bulletin board material to opponents, for example. Old wounds have a chance to heal. And the individuals themselves often see their playing or coaching days in a new light. That's why, in the following pages, you'll find Cazzie Russell speaking candidly about the most controversial moment of his U-M career. Tim McCormick tells us about the senior who took McCormick aside before his first college game and told the freshman to avoid shooting that season, to pass him the ball instead, so the senior could set a scoring record. Tom

Staton reveals what Johnny Orr said he would've done had Staton missed a key shot in the NCAA tournament. And several Wolverines will take you behind the scenes during Michigan's national championship run in 1989.

You'll also find a few contemporary quotes in the book, taken from newspapers and magazines. Those quotes will be clearly identified. Any quote in this book that doesn't cite a different source comes from an interview I did with that individual.

BUILDING THE HOUSE, 1960–1968

Fittingly, the hiring process for the man who'd lead the University of Michigan basketball team to its first two Final Four appearances began during the NCAA tournament—with a meeting of Michigan basketball alumni at a coaches' convention held in conjunction with the 1960 NCAA Final Four. According to former Wolverines player and coach Jim Skala, U-M athletic director Fritz Crisler told the assembled Michigan men that he would seek a new coach, after Bill Perigo led U-M to a 4-20 season in 1959–60 (officially, Perigo resigned shortly thereafter). Asked who should replace Perigo, Skala replied, "He's sitting right here. Dave Strack."

Strack was a high school basketball star in Indiana who became a three-year starter at Michigan. In a remarkable coincidence, Strack became the first U-M player to wear no. 33 and later coached the Wolverines' last no. 33. After a brief taste of pre-NBA professional basketball, Strack returned to Ann Arbor as an assistant coach from 1948 to 1958 and then left in 1959 to become head coach at the University of Idaho.

After accepting the Michigan job one year later, Strack hired Skala and Tom Jorgensen—another former U-M captain—as assistants, making Strack the first U-M hoops coach to have two full-time assistants. Skala calls Strack "a positive type of coach....I never saw [Strack] chastise, berate, put somebody down." Nevertheless, Strack believed in meticulous preparation. If the coach witnessed a player miss a layup in pregame warm-ups, for example, "it just drove him nuts," says George Pomey, who played under Strack for three years. "[Strack] said, 'If you're careless when there's nobody

Michigan head coach Dave Strack (center) flanked by his All-Americans: Bill Buntin (far left) and Cazzie Russell. *BL016892, Bentley Historical Library, University of Michigan.*

guarding you, how are you going to make a basket when you get in a game, when you've got somebody guarding you?'"

Strack also emphasized conditioning, which wasn't typical in that era, and expected his starters to be ready to play forty minutes. "I figured a player at that age could play a game with your normal timeouts without resting all the time," Strack explains.

When Strack's first team opened practice in October, he says that he "didn't have any master plan. I was happy to be back at Michigan. I didn't have a contract. I was on an annual basis you might say, but that didn't worry me either because I felt I could do the job.…I had great faith in Michigan having faith in me."

YOST FIELD HOUSE

Thanks to its mid-1960s success, the basketball team gained a new home later in the decade, and Yost Field House was eventually converted into a hockey arena. But in 1960, Yost was a forty-year-old, multi-purpose facility. The basketball court sat on a raised platform that was brought in for practices and

Preparing for a basketball game at Yost Field House, in 1960. *HS3024, Bentley Historical Library, University of Michigan.*

games. The roof leaked—sometimes during events, usually due to melting snow—while pigeons and occasionally bats flew in and nested among the rafters. The building was cold in the winter, and the lighting was poor. And yet some enjoyed the building's old-fashioned charms. Rudy Tomjanovich, who played in Yost with the 1966–67 freshman team, says that he "loved that place….The floor at Yost Field House was absolutely phenomenal as far as having spring in it. I was a good jumper, and I remember just loving how my legs felt on that floor."

ON-COURT STRUGGLES, OFF-COURT SUCCESS

Strack's first two teams were only marginally better than Perigo's last one, finishing 6-18 and 7-17, respectively, with a combined 7-21 Big Ten record. On the recruiting trail, however, Strack and his staff laid the groundwork for future success. Strack scored his initial recruiting coup shortly after

On the court, Michigan's basketball revival began with Bill Buntin. *BL008061, Bentley Historical Library, University of Michigan.*

gaining the U-M job, signing Indiana's player of the year, Bob Cantrell, sight unseen. Strack signed his first big recruiting class the following year, led by Bill Buntin, Larry Tregoning and Pomey, all of whom spent one year playing on the freshman team, as freshmen then were ineligible to play varsity basketball. Although Buntin was the least known of the trio, he became the key to Michigan's basketball renaissance.

Skala discovered Buntin two years earlier at a Detroit Northern High School game during Buntin's senior year, even though Buntin wasn't playing. At halftime, a tall Northern student—who appeared to be a team manager—walked on the court and began popping in hook shots at will. Skala—then coaching at Eastern Michigan—later asked Northern's coach about the mysterious manager. "And he said, 'You know, if I had him we'd win the state championship,'" Skala recalls. "But he said he broke his [leg] playing football and he can't play. And that was Bill Buntin."

Today, a player with Buntin's talent would be a coveted recruit by the age of fifteen or sixteen at the latest. At that time, however, there were no elite basketball camps, no recruiting-oriented media and, of course, no internet to share video of his play. So when Buntin missed his senior high school season due to the football injury, he was invisible on the recruiting scene to practically everyone—except Skala.

After Buntin's injury healed the following year, he began playing recreational basketball in Detroit. Skala, now coaching at U-M, rediscovered him, and Strack eventually invited Buntin to Ann Arbor. Buntin's visit included a trip to the campus Intramural Building, where some Michigan players—probably not by coincidence—were playing a pickup game, which Buntin joined. Strack and the coaches left, to avoid any suspicion that they'd set up what amounted to a team tryout. But Strack later got a full report from team captain Tom Cole, who said that Buntin was better than anyone he'd faced in the Big Ten that season, cementing Strack's decision to offer Buntin a scholarship. His signing, Strack says, was "the start of Michigan's resurgence in basketball."

At 6-foot-7 and 230 pounds, Buntin was undersized for a Big Ten center but made up for it with his strength and leaping ability. Buntin possessed good post moves—including the hook shot that impressed Skala—and a solid mid-range game. He was also a physical player and strong rebounder. But the tough guy disappeared when the games ended, as Buntin's good-natured charm helped build Michigan's team chemistry, and his home became the team's social center.

"He was a great individual," says Cazzie Russell, who played alongside Buntin for two seasons. "Just a tough-nosed guy, but underneath there's a big teddy bear. I think that's probably why I really loved him and really admired him so much, because he was a big kid having fun."

Upward

Buntin made an immediate impact as a sophomore, averaging 22.3 points and 15.7 rebounds per game. Just as important for Michigan, however, was Cantrell's development as a floor leader. After scoring 12.1 points per game the previous season, Cantrell shot less and passed more in each succeeding season, which helped keep the offense flowing and integrate players such as Buntin and Russell smoothly into the Wolverines' lineup. Cantrell also established the physical defensive style that became Michigan's trademark.

Pomey recalls a game against Western Michigan in which Cantrell held Manny Newsome, who averaged 32.7 points per game, to 10 points. "Bobby followed him all over the floor. He even wound up walking in [Western's] huddle with him one time. The coach got so mad he went after Cantrell on the floor.…It's just the way [Cantrell] was. He was a tough, hard-nose old bugger."

With Buntin leading the way, Michigan raced to an 8-1 pre–Big Ten start in 1962–63 and followed with a solid 8-6 conference campaign. Buntin led the Big Ten in rebounding and broke Michigan's one-season scoring mark with 534 points, although the record would be broken again the following year by the school's eighth, and last, player to wear no. 33.

CAZZIE GOES BLUE

Cazzie Lee Russell Jr. grew up on Chicago's South Side. A strong baseball player, Russell didn't play organized basketball until he entered George Washington Carver High School, where his destiny—and that of U-M basketball—was changed forever after varsity basketball coach Larry Hawkins spotted the 6-foot-2 Russell in the hallway. Hawkins brought Russell to the gym at the end of a school day and had him shoot some hoops. Young Cazzie was raw but impressive, and with Hawkins's encouragement, Russell joined the basketball team.

Russell didn't become a varsity starter until his junior year. But he'd blossomed sufficiently that he received more than fifty scholarship offers that season, with U-M joining the competition in Cazzie's senior year. "Of course Cazzie was Chicago's best high school player, and we recruited him," Strack says. "I didn't think he would be interested in us, but he was very interested in us." Russell eventually narrowed his choices to Michigan and the University of Cincinnati.

"When I think about the Michigan years, I know I was blessed because I was headed to Cincinnati, but it just so happened that the Lord just changed my mind," says Russell, who became an ordained minister in 1989. "Because [basketball Hall of Famer] Oscar Robertson came to my high school and tried to get me to go to Cincinnati."

Despite his admiration for NBA star Robertson, Russell wanted to play in the Big Ten. With Hawkins advising him to attend a strong academic school, Russell visited Ann Arbor and, most importantly, met Buntin. The two got along well until they decided to play billiards. As often happens when competitive personalities square off, the friendly game became serious, and Buntin "beat my tail," as Russell recalls. Buntin then told Russell that if he wanted a rematch, he'd have to enroll at Michigan. "I guess he realized I didn't like losing," Russell says.

If Buntin was a key factor in Cazzie's recruitment, creaky old Yost Field House apparently was not because Russell didn't tour the building until he

Cazzie Russell practices his shot at Yost Field House. *BL008685, Bentley Historical Library, University of Michigan.*

arrived in Ann Arbor for his freshman season. "I was on a [recruiting] visit, and Dave [Strack] said he lost the key," Russell says, "so I never had a chance to see the inside of Yost Field House."

Speaking forty-eight years after Russell's visit, Strack recalls that Cazzie "claims he didn't see the Field House. I'm not sure," he adds with a chuckle. "I think we showed him everything. They made a big story out of that, he said that I lost the key to get into the Field House—maybe it's true, I don't know. Makes a good story, though." Even without viewing his future home court, the chance to help rebuild the Wolverines' basketball program proved irresistible, and Russell chose Michigan.

On paper, the 6-foot-5½, 218-pound Russell was termed a guard in his first two varsity seasons. Defensively, however, he'd generally cover an opposing forward. On the offensive end, Cazzie was everywhere. He often brought the ball upcourt. He'd shoot from the perimeter on one possession, drive the lane and dish off to a teammate on another and then post up a smaller guard whenever possible. He had the finesse to hit perimeter shots from what today would be 3-point range and the strength to drive the lane, absorb contact and still put the ball through the hoop. "Caz was the first prototype large guard," teammate Oliver Darden says.

Russell not only developed a solid understanding of the game—it's no surprise that he became a coach when his playing career ended—but he also worked as hard as anyone on the team, even to a point where U-M coaches occasionally interrupted one of his off-hours practice sessions and sent him home to rest.

Despite all that practice time, Russell's mechanics weren't always conventional. Rather than shoot with a traditional arc, for example, "Cazzie's shot was very flat," Pomey recalls, "but thankfully nobody tried to change him because he practiced so much that it was OK for him." The only thing Russell didn't do at U-M was take on the toughest defensive assignments, as Strack didn't want to risk his offensive star getting in foul trouble.

Russell was a starter from the beginning of his sophomore season. Buntin remained at center, Cantrell started in the backcourt and Larry Tregoning—an excellent defender who also possessed good shooting range—was the small forward. Oliver Darden, also a sophomore in 1964, played the power forward spot. The Detroit native was a great leaper who did much of the physical dirty work that helped open the floor for Russell and others. But like Cazzie, Darden's first sport growing up was baseball. As he grew to 6-foot-7, however, Darden gravitated to basketball. Also like Cazzie, contact with Buntin helped persuade Darden to attend U-M. But he particularly enjoyed Michigan's most famous sports trademark.

"I loved the football helmets," Darden says. "Those helmets were just wonderful, they were so unique. And they still are."

When he reached the U-M varsity, Darden understood the team's hierarchy. He and teammates such as Cantrell, Tregoning and Pomey accepted their supplementary roles, which included guarding their opponents' key scorers, rebounding and getting the ball to Russell and Buntin. This attitude helped the Wolverines blend into a harmonious unit. And nobody was more pleased than Buntin, who'd done his best to recruit his new, standout teammates just a year earlier. "He embraced them all," Skala says.

Meanwhile, Russell's respect for Buntin grew, beginning in Cazzie's freshman season. "My relationship with Billy was a good one," Russell says. "I had to make sure that he knew that the reason that we were going to be successful was because he was in the middle. And that was very important. No matter what people said, the publicity I got, it didn't make any difference. If he didn't do what he was supposed to do, we were not going to win."

But Russell also recognized Buntin's weakness: a tendency to gain weight—a flaw that would haunt the big man after his college career ended. So Russell tried to motivate Buntin to remain slim. Russell told Buntin bluntly that Michigan wouldn't succeed "if you're lazy and you're not in shape." But Russell also recognized that Buntin liked joining Michigan's fast break. "He loved getting easy layups and dunks," Russell recalls. So he encouraged Buntin to stay in shape to run the floor. And if Buntin did so, Cazzie promised, "I'll get you the ball."

Bloody Nose Lane

As the 1963–64 season opened, Michigan basketball was blossoming. Nationally, U-M was ranked eighth in the preseason. Locally, an unprecedented fourteen thousand students applied for season tickets. For the first time, Michigan students had to stand in line to enter Yost Field House. But the wait was worth it. Russell debuted with a 30-point performance and led the Wolverines to a 5-0 start. They were ranked second and third, respectively, in the two national polls as they prepared for their first-ever game against Duke, which would become perhaps U-M's biggest non-conference rival.

The defending ACC champs were ranked fifth when they invaded Yost in 1964. Duke played a tight zone, keying on Buntin, but the strategy backfired as the Wolverines shot 60 percent from the field on their way to an 83–67 victory. In addition to its hot shooting, Michigan was physically dominant, out-rebounding Duke 61–35, led by Buntin's 18.

The Wolverines then traveled west for the Los Angeles Classic. They defeated NYU before losing their first game of the year, to no. 3 UCLA, 98–80. The smaller but much quicker Bruins used a zone press to force 21 turnovers and prevented U-M from taking advantage of its size.

Michigan entered the Big Ten season as the favorite and, after opening with two victories, firmly established its credentials by trouncing three-time defending champ Ohio State, 82–64. The Buckeyes tried to key on Russell, but he still burned them on both ends of the court, scoring 27 points and adding five steals, while the Buckeyes' first six personal fouls were committed by Cazzie's defenders.

As the season progressed, Michigan's reputation for physical play grew. All the Wolverines played tough, and ballhandlers who dared to venture into the paint faced a gauntlet that Strack named "Bloody Nose Lane."

"Yeah, I did [invent the nickname]," Strack says, with a hint of regret. "Well, it was just that, we felt that area under the basket belonged to the defensive team and you came in there at your own risk."

While Darden and other Wolverines did play physical defense, Pomey says that Buntin truly inspired the nickname. "He was just as strong as an ox," Pomey recalls. "The reputation of Bloody Nose Lane wasn't really what he was like as a person. But when he put on his uniform he guarded the center pretty well." With physical play as its hallmark and cheering crowds now filling Yost, Michigan rolled to an 8-2 conference mark, tied for first with Ohio State.

The next contest became Michigan's most lopsided victory of the year but also the costliest. In a 103–59 thrashing of visiting Wisconsin, Cantrell accidentally stepped on Russell's foot, straining tendons and ligaments in Russell's ankle. Although he played in every remaining contest except the NCAA consolation game, Cazzie was never fully healthy for the rest of the season.

Sore ankle or not, Russell didn't lose his scoring touch. He netted 28 in a victory against Illinois to break Buntin's one-season scoring record. Ohio State also won, leaving both teams at 10-2 in conference play with two games remaining.

In 1964, each conference could only place one squad in the 25-team NCAA tournament field. Under Big Ten rules, if two teams tied for the championship, the school that went to the tournament most recently was eliminated, and Ohio State had represented the Big Ten in 1963. So when Michigan beat Iowa, 69–61, while Michigan State edged Ohio State, Michigan clinched the second NCAA bid in school history.

The Wolverines had to settle for a tie with OSU after Purdue upset Michigan, 81–79, at Yost, leaving both Michigan and Ohio State at 11-3 in conference play. But the co-championship gave U-M its first conference basketball title since 1948.

Final Four-ward

Second-ranked Michigan, 20-4 overall, began NCAA Mideast Regional play in Minneapolis. As the Big Ten representative, U-M automatically earned a first-round bye—the modern NCAA tournament seeding system wasn't in place yet—and faced eighth-ranked Loyola in the second round. In its first NCAA appearance in sixteen years, Michigan faced the defending national champ, which returned four starters from its title-winning squad.

The 21-5 Ramblers opened an early 6-point lead before Michigan began to slow Loyola's fast-break offense and dominate Bloody Nose Lane. (For the game, the taller and stronger Wolverines out-rebounded Loyola 47–37 and blocked seven shots.) Michigan took a 43–36 lead into halftime, even though the Ramblers had held Russell to four points.

Russell handled the ball more frequently in the second half, leading U-M to a seemingly comfortable 74–64 lead. In the final minutes, however, Michigan's foul trouble helped Loyola rally. To protect his starters, Strack switched from his favored man-to-man to a zone. A late 6–1 run drew the Ramblers within two points before Cantrell secured the 84–80 victory with a pair of free throws with 10 seconds remaining, giving Michigan its first-ever non-consolation NCAA tournament victory.

Russell had rested following the Purdue contest and looked healthy against Loyola, until he came up limping after scoring on a baseline drive in the second half. Nevertheless, he was ready to go the following day against Ohio University, which had shocked Kentucky in the regional semifinal. Michigan led 32–27 at halftime but couldn't shake the MAC champs early in the second half. It was 43-all with 12:43 left when Michigan finally distanced itself with six straight points. The Wolverines soon slowed the game and wrapped it up at the foul line to advance to their first Final Four with a 69–57 victory.

Russell used the next five days off to rest, performing only shooting drills, but still wasn't 100 percent when Michigan faced third-ranked Duke in the national semifinals.

Although U-M had whipped the Blue Devils in December, Duke was much stronger in March. The ACC champions entered the game 25-4 and now featured 6-foot-10 Jay Buckley at center, which made Duke a better rebounding team. Michigan had dominated the boards by almost a two-to-one margin in the teams' regular season contest, but the Blue Devils out-rebounded U-M 46–45 in the semifinal. In particular, Duke took care of its own defensive boards, which removed a staple of Michigan's offense—the put-back—while triggering the Blue Devils' running game.

Russell sank his first five shots, as the teams exchanged leads for much of the opening half, before Duke began pulling away. Employing an aggressive man-to-man defense, the Blue Devils forced 12 U-M turnovers in the first half, while committing just three of their own, on the way to a 48–39 lead after 20 minutes.

Michigan never made a serious run in the second half. U-M pulled within 71–64 with fewer than 10 minutes remaining but drew no closer in a 91–80 defeat.

Russell scored 31 on 13-for-19 shooting, but other aspects of his game—including rebounding and defense—suffered due to his foot injury. "Cazzie was playing on one leg," Skala says. "He just wasn't 100 percent." Russell didn't play in the consolation game the next day, as Michigan defeated Kansas State, 100–90, to finish 23-5 overall, no. 3 in the country.

Number One

With four starters and most of its key reserves back, Michigan began the 1964–65 season as the consensus no. 1 team in the nation, with defending champion UCLA ranked second. Michigan's key graduation loss was Cantrell, the fiery captain, who was replaced by Pomey. In addition to defending the opponents' top guards, Pomey ran Michigan's offense and distributed the ball to the scorers. And the Wolverines did plenty of scoring.

As of 2023, only three U-M teams have averaged more than 90 points per game for a full season. The 1989 team averaged 91.7 while playing with a 3-point line and a shot clock that prevented opponents from stalling. But Michigan's other two 90-points-plus seasons came back to back in 1964–65 (90.4 points per game) and 1965–66 (91.9), when college basketball lacked both a shot clock and a 3-point arc.

Michigan's success in those earlier two seasons began with Strack's up-tempo style on both ends of the floor. On defense, the Wolverines pressed frequently. On offense, "We took the first good shot off our pattern offense that we could," Pomey explains. "And the offense basically was predicated on getting good, wide-open shots and a lot of layups, with back-cuts and things like that."

Strack's strategy emphasized shooting from within 15 feet. With no 3-point line, there was little reason to take deeper, lower-percentage shots. "We took the fast break whenever it presented itself," Skala says. "I think we could run with most people [except UCLA]….Naturally we featured

George Pomey was
the floor leader
for some of U-M's
highest-scoring
teams. *BL016885,
Bentley Historical
Library, University of
Michigan.*

getting Cazzie shots, we featured getting the ball in low and we were a very
strong backboard team. I mean we pounded those offensive and defensive
backboards."

Strack preferred man-to-man defense, mixing in an occasional zone,
usually to protect a player in foul trouble. But Michigan occasionally used a
trapping half-court zone in 1964–65, with Pomey on the point, similar to a
modern 1-3-1 look.

In the second game of the '64–65 season, Michigan gained some payback
by ending Duke's 27-game home winning streak with an 86–79 victory.
Following an upset loss at Nebraska, which dropped U-M to second in the
polls, Michigan faced no. 1 Wichita State in a game played at Cobo Hall,
then the home of the NBA Detroit Pistons.

The contest lived up to its billing, featuring 15 lead changes and seven ties.
The second half was close all the way, with Wichita holding an 85–83 lead
before Russell drained a long jumper to tie the game at 85 with 28 seconds

remaining. But as Wichita tried to play for the last shot, a pass bounced off leading scorer Dave Stallworth's leg and went out of bounds with four seconds left.

Russell then in-bounded to Pomey, who dribbled upcourt quickly, while Wichita took its eyes off the prize. "There was no way I was going to shoot a long-range shot and have any chance of making it," Pomey says. "Yet…I dribbled up the court, then two guys come over towards me and he's wide open in the middle."

"He" was Russell, who took Pomey's pass, dribbled twice and fired from beyond the free throw circle. The buzzer sounded, and then the ball swished through the net for a Michigan victory.

Russell explains that at crucial moments, "Some guys want the ball, other guys do not. I guess I was just one of the guys that wanted the ball.…My mindset was not, 'Oh, what if I miss?' Oh, no-no-no-no. My mindset was, 'Let me get my hands on it, and let's see what happens.'"

Cazzie had "what I call the confidence that borders on arrogance," Darden says. "And I think that's what the true superstars have to have. It's that mentality [of], 'Give me the ball when the game's on the line. I'll shoot it.' Although I didn't appreciate it as much then, as I look back in hindsight, that's what you need when you have a superstar, or a guy who can carry the team."

Russell versus Bradley, Part I

Michigan traveled to the Holiday Festival at New York's Madison Square Garden in late December for a dream match-up between the nation's top two college players: Cazzie Russell and Princeton's Bill Bradley.

Bradley, Russell's future NBA teammate—as well as a future U.S. senator and presidential candidate—was probably the best-known college player in the country at that time. Like Russell, the 6-foot-5 Bradley played a variety of roles for the Tigers. Unlike Russell, Bradley was far superior to all his teammates on a young Princeton squad.

The first half of the showdown belonged to the Ivy Leaguer. Bradley scored 23 points, including Princeton's final 12, as the Tigers took a 39–37 halftime edge. Only Buntin's 19-point effort kept Michigan close in the first 20 minutes. Russell was held to 2-for-8 shooting by Princeton's Don Rodenbach—and possibly by Russell's floppy sneaker when part of the sole disconnected from his shoe's upper portion. With no extra shoes on hand,

U-M assistant trainer Len Paddock ran two blocks from the arena to the team's hotel to retrieve a second pair.

Michigan went to a press in the second half, but Bradley handled it himself by bringing the ball upcourt—and he continued to score almost at will. Meanwhile, the Wolverines went scoreless for the first 4:46 of the half. The only good news for Michigan was the arrival of Russell's second pair of shoes and Rodenbach's foul trouble, which forced him from the game. Nevertheless, Princeton was in control, leading 75–63 with 4:37 left, when Bradley fouled out. "They had us beat," says Pomey. "We should've never won. [But] Bradley, as brilliant a guy as he was mentally, committed his fifth foul reaching around the back of [Darden] in a lazy situation."

Bradley's fifth foul turned the tide, even though Buntin had already fouled out and Darden was about to follow. Princeton had increased its lead to 77–63 with 3:33 left when Michigan went to a full-court, man-to-man press. Without Bradley, the Tigers struggled to cross half court, and Michigan gained complete control. The only question was whether the Wolverines had time to erase Princeton's cushion.

Princeton led 78–68 with 2:08 left but wouldn't score again. Michigan tallied 10 points in the next 1:17, scoring three times off Princeton's backcourt turnovers. Pomey set up the tying basket by stealing the ball and feeding guard John Thompson for a layup. Russell then intercepted a pass with 36 seconds remaining. Michigan held the ball for 34 seconds before Russell sank another buzzer-beater—a 12-footer from the left side to win the showdown, 80–78.

Michigan closed the game with a 17–1 run in the final 3:33, including nine points by Russell, who finished with 27. Bradley scored 41 of Princeton's 78 points. After the game, he told his teammates that they would meet Michigan again in the NCAA tournament.

Defending the Big Ten Title

A confident Michigan entered the Big Ten as a solid favorite, and the Wolverines played up to expectations, winning the tough conference with a 13-1 mark. Indeed, no. 1–ranked Michigan lost one fewer contest against Big Ten competition than did no. 2–ranked UCLA, which dropped games to Illinois and Iowa.

Michigan's toughest Big Ten victory was a double-overtime comeback win at Indiana. Both teams entered the contest 15-2 overall. Seventh-ranked Indiana was 5-2 in conference play, while Michigan was 7-0. But the Wolverines appeared headed for their first conference loss, trailing the Hoosiers 81–74 with 56 seconds remaining. "The Indiana fans, they were chanting, 'We're number one! We're number one! We're number one!'" Skala recalls. But the exuberance was premature, as Tregoning capped a 7–0 run with two free throws to send the contest into OT, and then a Russell put-back forced a second overtime period. A pair of Russell free throws with 45 seconds left in the second overtime put U-M ahead 96–95, and then Buntin blocked a shot at the buzzer to preserve the victory.

The game was over, but the competitive fire remained, as Skala offered a belated response to the Indiana fans' late-game taunts by raising his index finger in the traditional "We're no. 1" gesture. As he walked off the court, "I was physically assaulted" by fans, Skala relates. "I had my coat torn off, and in the meantime, Strack got into a contest with Lou Watson, who was [Indiana head coach] Branch McCracken's assistant coach. And Lou was ready to take Strack on....I got down to the locker room after all that had transpired, and Strack said, 'Where the hell were you when I needed ya?'"

After wrapping up conference play, Michigan headed to its second consecutive NCAA tournament as the Big Ten's undisputed champion.

The Not-So-Big Dance

Darden notes that the 1960s NCAA tournament bore "no comparison at all" to the Big Dance of the twenty-first century. In 1965, for example, just 23 teams qualified for the event. "We played on Friday-Saturday, Friday-Saturday. Two weekends. That was it. So you really did not have the hoop and the hype you have nowadays."

Top-ranked Michigan opened Mideast Regional play in Lexington, Kentucky, by trouncing Dayton, 98–71, setting up a regional final against fifth-ranked Vanderbilt, the SEC champ. Led by 6-foot-11 future NBA center Clyde Lee, the Commodores entered the contest 24-3 and played Michigan tough, leading the Wolverines 75–72 before Russell took charge. Cazzie scored 11 points in the final five minutes to help U-M take an 85–81 lead with 58 seconds left. John Miller pulled Vandy within two with 52 seconds remaining, but with no shot clock, the Commodores were forced to foul to prevent Michigan from stalling out the game.

The strategy might've worked, as Michigan missed the front ends of three consecutive 1-and-1 opportunities. But Darden rebounded two of the misses, and Pomey snatched the other. Darden was then fouled with three seconds left and sank both free throws, making Vanderbilt's last-second hoop irrelevant as Michigan prevailed, 87–85. Michigan was off to its second consecutive Final Four, this time as the favorite.

While Michigan advanced after a close call, its next opponent had shocked and destroyed fourth-ranked Providence in the East Regional final, 109–69, thanks to 41 points from its senior All-American, Bill Bradley.

Russell versus Bradley, Part II

An ecstatic Bradley had made his dream come true, practically willing Princeton, now 22-5, into a rematch with the Wolverines. Bradley played well in his final meaningful college game, but the Wolverines were better prepared for his magic.

Bradley still got his points early in the contest, as Princeton took a 34–29 lead. But the Wolverines went on an 11–2 run to grab a 40–36 halftime advantage, behind Buntin's 16 points. Ominously for the Tigers, Bradley owned three fouls at the break. After Bradley fouled Darden for his fourth personal early in the second half, Princeton went to a zone to protect its star. Strack then moved Russell to the high post and let him shoot over the zone, or pass to open teammates, and the Wolverines began pulling away. U-M led 75–67 when Bradley fouled out with 5:04 remaining. Unlike their previous matchup, Bradley's early exit determined only the victory margin, not the victor, as the Wolverines cruised to a 93–76 win.

Led by Russell's 28 points and a 56–32 rebounding advantage, Michigan reached its first NCAA Final and faced defending champ UCLA. The second-ranked Bruins entered the final 27-2, with only those losses to Illinois and Iowa—against whom Michigan was a combined 3-0—to stain their record. But while the Wolverines were playing a faster-paced game that season, UCLA was still quicker than Michigan.

Russell scored 12 early points as U-M took a 20–13 lead eight minutes into the contest. Then the UCLA zone press began wearing the Wolverines down. "We tried not to get into a running game with them," Skala says. "That quickness and their press and everything else, it just got to us."

The press did what was intended: force turnovers and ignite UCLA's offense. Led by 6-foot guard Gail Goodrich, the Bruins tied the game at 24 midway through the half, as Michigan had increasing trouble advancing over midcourt. "Against a team like that you can't turn the ball over," Russell says. "As a matter of fact, the whole purpose of the press was to up-tempo the game. Since we were bigger, they felt like they could outrun us."

Defensively, after doing well to hold Bradley to 29 points, Pomey's reward was going head-to-head with Goodrich when Michigan played man-to-man. "Goodrich was completely different than Bradley was," Pomey says. "[Goodrich] was just so good with the ball and so quick and able to penetrate and get to the basket…you didn't know where he was going. He didn't ever do two [similar] things in a row."

UCLA ended the half on a 12–1 run for a 47–34 lead. Shockingly, the smaller Bruins out-rebounded U-M in the first half 19–17. At halftime Strack told U-M "to go back and run faster, jump higher, and rebound better." But Goodrich grabbed the opening tap of the second half and dashed in for a layup, foreshadowing more of the same.

Strack tried to turn the tables with a half-court trap and succeeded briefly, as Michigan forced some UCLA turnovers and pulled within a dozen points midway through the half. But the Bruins began playing keepaway and—with no shot clock—forced Michigan into desperation mode. As a result, Buntin, Tregoning and Darden all fouled out—each drawing his fifth foul while chasing Goodrich—as UCLA built a 20-point lead on its way to a 91–80 victory. "They were a little quicker than we were," Strack says. "I'm not sure we should've lost the game, but we did.… We couldn't handle Goodrich, really."

Goodrich led the Bruins with 42 points, sinking 18 of 20 free throws. Michigan's offense, led by Russell's 28 points, wasn't shabby, but the Wolverines were out-rebounded 34–33 and grabbed just nine offensive boards, normally a staple of their game. "That's a game I'd like to forget," says Strack—pain still evident in his voice, forty-five years after the fact. "They were good. [Coach John] Wooden was very good. Goodrich was excellent.…That was a heartbreaking loss."

Filling Buntin's Shoes

Strack's first great recruiting class having graduated, his second stellar class stepped up to lead the 1965–66 squad. Without Buntin, the team was less muscular, but it was quicker. John Clawson replaced Tregoning and became the second-leading scorer on the highest-scoring team in U-M history. John Thompson took Pomey's spot as the lead guard and key defender. But Strack's biggest problem was filling Buntin's shoes, as junior

Craig Dill, and then senior Jim Myers, tried to replace, in Russell's words, "that mad man in the middle."

It took a while to adjust to Buntin's absence, as Michigan's 6-4 non-conference record indicates. The pre-conference highlight was Russell's school-record 45 points in a victory over San Francisco. But the Wolverines didn't let their non-conference struggles affect their Big Ten play. Indeed, U-M opened the conference season by winning at Ohio State for the first time in nineteen years, 83–78, on the way to a 5-0 Big Ten start.

A loss to Illinois broke Michigan's 16-game home winning streak and left U-M and Michigan State tied atop the Big Ten standings at 5-1. The Wolverines then beat Indiana before going on an unprecedented scoring binge against visiting Wisconsin. Michigan attacked defensively with a zone press and sank 16 of its first 20 shots on the way to a 61–40 halftime lead, and then added 59 more points in the second half, winning 120–102.

Michigan set or tied seven school or conference records against Wisconsin, some of which only lasted a week, as Michigan destroyed Purdue in the following game, 128–94, overcoming a Big Ten record 57 points from Purdue's Dave Schellhase. Michigan featured balanced scoring led by Russell (28 points), Clawson (27), Myers (22) and Darden (21).

Although Michigan dropped its next contest at Iowa, the Wolverines then scored at least 103 points in each of their next three games to clinch their third consecutive Big Ten title. The final game of Michigan's late-season winning streak was also the last home game for the five starting seniors. "I can recall standing there," Darden recalls, "basically with tears in my eyes

Oliver Darden was an outstanding power forward before that term existed. *BL019624, Bentley Historical Library, University of Michigan.*

and thinking, 'Where have the four years gone?'" Russell says he "didn't sleep well the night before, realizing that it was all over. [But the game] was really great. The guys said they were going to turn me loose.…I think it was sort of, I would say, a compliment to the fact that I really considered myself a team player and did what I was told to do" throughout his college career.

With the conference title there for the taking following an MSU loss earlier in the day, Russell was indeed turned loose, and he took full advantage. Sinking 20 of 34 shots, plus 8 of 11 free throws, he broke his own single-game school scoring mark with 48 points in a 105–92 victory over Northwestern.

Russell, Darden and Strack were lifted on the shoulders of players and fans following the game. Some fans remained in Yost for an hour after the contest, as if they didn't want Michigan's golden basketball era to end. The end was indeed near, but Cazzie and company had one shining moment remaining.

Cazzie's Last Miracle

The 17-7 Wolverines began Mideast Regional play at Iowa City against Ohio Valley Conference champion Western Kentucky, which was 24-2. The no. 10 Hilltoppers battled no. 9 Michigan to the end, as Western Kentucky's zone defense slowed Michigan's attack. Michigan tried to stall with a 1-point lead and 3:50 remaining, hoping to force the Hilltoppers to foul. Instead, the Wolverines turned the ball over several times in the closing minutes and trailed 79–78 with 14 seconds remaining and Western Kentucky's Wayne Chapman at the foul line. Chapman missed, but Russell and Greg Smith then tied each other up going for the rebound, so a jump ball was called (the alternate possession rule was still fifteen years in the future). Unfortunately for Michigan, the 6-foot-5 Smith was clearly a better leaper than Russell, who had little hope of winning the tap—and he knew it.

"I knew he was a good jumper, and I noticed how antsy he was to go up for the ball," Russell says. "So when they threw the ball up, I just made it look like he had jumped into me, and they called a foul. [Western Kentucky] said that I acted on it. When I went up for the ball, he just kind of jumped into me, and I kind of faked it a little bit, too." After the game, referee Steve Honzo explained that he saw Smith jump into Russell, making a call that could still upset some veteran Hilltoppers' fans decades after the fact.

But Cazzie still had to sink the 1-and-1 with 11 seconds left. "Every kid dreams of this, but the question is, are you ready when reality sets in?"

Russell says. "And here we are, 1-and-1. If you don't make the first, it's over....The first one went straight through to tie the game. And a lot of people have asked me about that—'What were you thinking?' I said, 'I wasn't thinking anything, man. Just thinking that I had to make these free throws.'...The first one went through and the second one rattled, and I said, 'Don't you dare come out of there!'" The ball listened to Cazzie, and Michigan had an 80–79 victory.

The Wolverines advanced to their third consecutive regional final, but this time they were underdogs against no. 1 Kentucky, the SEC champion, which entered the contest 25-1. Kentucky coach Adolph Rupp famously preferred man-to-man defense, but after witnessing Michigan struggle with Western Kentucky's zone, the wily Rupp had a surprise for the Wolverines.

"Old Adolph Rupp swore that zone defenses should be outlawed for college basketball," Skala recalls. Nevertheless, Rupp "played 1-3-1 zone against us. Which shouldn't have bothered us, but we just had a bad shooting night and it did bother us."

Like the UCLA teams that had frustrated U-M, Kentucky was a small, quick squad with no starter taller than 6-foot-5. The Wildcats controlled the opening 20 minutes with their trapping zone and led 42–32 at halftime. Russell then tried to put Michigan on his back one more time. Scoring 13 points in the first eight minutes of the half, he sparked U-M to a 53–52 lead. Kentucky quickly regained the edge, and while the Wolverines pulled within 57–56 and 59–58, they never led again. Kentucky stretched its lead to 70–62 with five minutes left and held on for an 84–77 victory.

Russell was named the NCAA player of the year for 1965–66, a first-ever honor for Michigan. He was also the Big Ten's player of the year for the second consecutive season and was a first team All-America and All-Big Ten choice for the third straight year. Russell was voted the team's most valuable player each of his three varsity years (he shared the 1965 honor with Buntin). He broke the U-M season scoring record for the third consecutive season as a senior, finishing with 800 points. Only Glen Rice has ever done better at U-M, with 949 points in 1988–89, while playing 11 more games than Russell. Cazzie averaged a school record 30.8 points per game as a senior, while shooting a career-best 51.8 percent from the field and grabbing 8.3 rebounds per contest.

As of 2023, Russell still leads Michigan in career scoring average with 27.1 points per game, while averaging 8.4 rebounds per contest. Assists weren't tracked before the mid-1970s, but Cazzie would likely have an impressive assist total as well. But perhaps most importantly, as the face of Michigan basketball in the mid-1960s, he represented the university with humility and shared credit with his teammates.

"I came at, I guess, an opportune time," Russell says, "because Michigan was basically known as a football school. So to be a part of history in terms of having success and having played and being considered [an icon], it's a very humbling feeling, when you realize there were a lot of great players [at Michigan]. Obviously, I had a chance to make an impression first. Sometimes when you get there on the ground floor you get a chance to put your best foot forward."

Strack adds that while "you couldn't replace Cazzie…we had a lot of good players there….So I just came into a group of big, strong, players who could run and shoot and do the whole thing. We just didn't get the last milestone."

"Everybody knew their roles, and that, to me, was the key to our success," Darden says. He feels that his Wolverines group was "the most celebrated team that Michigan's ever had, even though we didn't win the championship like the 1989 group did, and we didn't get the hype that the Fab Five got. But I think that overall as a team, I don't think we can be beat."

Russell was selected by the New York Knicks as the NBA's first overall draft pick in 1966. He played twelve years in the NBA, teaming with old foe Bradley to help the Knicks win the 1970 NBA championship. Russell went on to coach at the high school, college and professional levels. No Michigan player has worn his no. 33 since he left school. The jersey was officially retired in 1993 and was the first U-M jersey to hang from the rafters in Crisler Arena. In 2011, he became the first Wolverine to be inducted into the National Collegiate Basketball Hall of Fame.

THE HOUSE THAT CAZZIE BUILT

Strack's final two seasons behind Michigan's bench resembled his first two, as the Wolverines won just 19 of 48 games. Strack's final season, 1967–68, brought two major changes that had a lasting impact on Michigan basketball. The first was the decision to hire a new lead assistant, which brought Strack into contact with former University of Wisconsin assistant Johnny Orr, who had left coaching to go into business.

"He says both of his assistants are leaving him," Orr recalls. "He says he's looking for a coach. And I say, 'Gosh, I see all the [Illinois] high school coaches, to sell insurance.' And he said, 'Well, if you find me a good one let me know, will you?' And so I said, 'I sure will.' And so about a month later

I called him up and I said, 'I found you a good one.' And he said, 'Who's that?' And I said, 'Me.'"

After persuading AD Fritz Crisler to let him hire a coach with no U-M ties, Strack brought Orr in as Michigan's lead assistant.

The second major change in 1967 was the completion of the basketball team's new home. The $7.2 million facility, designed by former U-M football player Dan Dworsky, was originally called the Events Building. But during construction, fans began referring to the rising arena as "Cazzie's Castle" or, more commonly, "The House that Cazzie Built." When Russell learned what fans and fellow students were calling the building, "It was very humbling," says Russell, who never played in the arena while at U-M. "But I did play [there] the following year when the Knicks and the Pistons played an exhibition game, and it was really great," Russell adds.

Rudy T

The highlight of the 1967–68 season was the varsity debut of Michigan's first post-Cazzie star: Rudy Tomjanovich, who'd grown up in Hamtramck, Michigan, watching Strack's teams dominate the Big Ten. "So I became a fan of those guys," Tomjanovich says, "and especially Cazzie." Meeting Russell was a highlight of Tomjanovich's recruitment. Later, the Michigan staff sent him an autographed Cazzie photo that he treasured. "I remember shaking his hand," Tomjanovich says. "Here I was, taller than him, but he had a wide, big hand. I was a skinny high school kid, and I was really impressed by him.…To me there was nobody that could compare to Cazzie. I had his autographed picture under some glass on a coffee table at home. I had heard about his work ethic and how he stayed after and practiced when everybody was gone, and I did the same thing. He was my role model."

At a slim 6-foot-8, Tomjanovich should've played forward, as he later did in his stellar NBA career. But Michigan could never pair him with a dominant big man, so Tomjanovich was essentially an undersized center for three years—albeit a big man who spent much of his time on the perimeter. Yet somehow, when shots were missed, there was Tomjanovich around the basket, positioned skillfully and scrapping for every loose ball.

"He was just a great, great shooter right off the bat," says Pomey, who was a U-M assistant coach at the time. "Long, long arms, and he just really had a nose for the ball. It wasn't that it was always just his jumping ability, but he really, really knew [how to rebound], and that's not something you can teach anybody. He just had a natural instinct, if somebody took a shot, where the ball was going to be."

A school-record crowd of 12,729 saw Michigan play its first game in the Events Building on December 2, 1967, in a 96–79 loss against Kentucky. Rudy T—as his NBA jersey would later read—led Michigan with 17 points and pulled down a school-record 27 rebounds in his debut.

"I was so excited in that game," Tomjanovich recalls. "I remember I shot a jump shot from the free throw line; I shot it so hard that I got my own offensive rebound at the free throw line....I also had 13 blocked shots, but they didn't keep it on the stats sheet."

After Michigan's season ended, with an 11-13 record, Strack began preparing for what he thought would be his ninth season behind Michigan's bench. In reality, he'd coached his last game. "I was blessed with great players, good assistants and had great support, if you attended any of those games at Ann Arbor in those years," Strack says. "So I had everything going for me."

Farewell, Bill Buntin

Bill Buntin was a first-round NBA draft pick, third overall, by the Pistons in 1965, but he reported to the team overweight and never got back into top playing shape. He appeared in 42 games in Detroit before being cut prior to his second season.

While playing a pickup game at Detroit's Cathedral High School on May 9, 1968, Buntin told friends that he felt sick. According to a *Detroit News* article, Buntin said he was going outside for a "breath of fresh air." By the time he was found, Buntin had collapsed with an apparent heart attack. The twenty-six-year-old Buntin, married with three children, was dead.

"I was so hurt when I heard that he had passed," Russell says. "And I just cried because his final autopsy weight was like 280, 285. He did have a struggle."

U-M eventually named its team Most Valuable Player award after Buntin. Four decades after Buntin's college career ended, after Michigan had lifted four jerseys to the Crisler Arena rafters, Strack lobbied successfully to add Buntin to the pantheon. In January 2006, Strack ventured from his retirement home in Arizona to attend the ceremony honoring Buntin's no. 22. The two men who'd sparked Michigan's basketball renaissance were, in a way, reunited at last.

ON THE RUN, 1968–1973

Johnny Orr eventually left U-M as the winningest basketball coach in school history. But his degree of success—and his ultimate decision to leave Michigan, rather than Michigan firing him—seemed unlikely through much of his first five years as U-M's head coach, during which Orr suffered numerous slings and arrows directed by outraged fans and media. "My first couple, three years there weren't very good," Orr admits, adding, with his characteristic humor, that he was so unpopular that "when I went to the supermarket the checkout woman would leave." During the height of that public displeasure, a candidate ran for U-M student government on a "Dump Orr" platform. And won. More on him later.

Many, including Orr, were shocked that he became the head coach in 1968, mainly because Strack, despite back-to-back losing seasons, seemed secure in his job. Then Fritz Crisler retired as Michigan's athletic director and was replaced by Don Canham.

Canham was a former U-M track and field athlete and coach who'd become a successful businessman. Even before his appointment as AD was announced, Canham made his first major coaching hire.

Orr recalls being in Strack's office when Canham entered and took Strack aside. Ten minutes later, Orr was asked to join the meeting. "So I went over there, and Don says, 'Johnny, I'm the new athletic director.' And I said, 'Well, congratulations, Don, that's terrific.' I said, 'Whoo man, are you really?' 'Yeah,' and he says, 'Dave's going to be my business manager.' And I didn't know whether Dave wanted to do that or not, so I said, 'Is that what you want to do, Dave?' because he was my boss. And he says, 'That's what I'm going to do.' I said, 'Well, good.' And [Canham] says, 'And we're going to hire you as our basketball coach. What do you think you're worth?' I said, '$18,500.' And he says, 'Ohhh, $15,000 is as high as I can go.' I said, 'I'll take it.'"

That was it. No search committee. No long, drawn-out hiring process. Just quick decisions by three men that set the course of Michigan basketball for the remainder of the century, as every departing head coach during that time would pass the torch to one of his assistants.

Orr, an Illinois native, was a multi-sport athlete in high school and college (University of Illinois and then Beloit College) who then played one season in the NBA. His coaching résumé included four years as a Wisconsin assistant and three years as head coach at the University of Massachusetts before he joined the U-M staff the previous year.

Breaking a Barrier

The forty-one-year-old Orr retained George Pomey as one assistant but also hired Fred Snowden, a successful high school coach from Detroit Northwestern, as his lead assistant, making Snowden the first Black coach in Big Ten basketball history. "I just knew him in high school, and I really respected him," Orr says. "He was really a disciplinarian, and he really had good teams.…Freddie and I were great friends. And he was sharp, man. A great recruiter, everything."

In 1968, having a Black assistant coach on a mostly White team could've caused friction. But according to Dan Fife—who played for the Orr-Snowden tandem for three years—neither the players nor Snowden had any problem with the arrangement. "Snowden was extremely savvy about stuff, how to deal with [racial matters]," Fife recalls. "If he had a race issue, he never brought it out. It seemed like he just took the high road to everything."

Ernest Johnson, who played two varsity seasons when Snowden was coaching, says that Snowden was important to him and to his fellow African American players. "It's such a cultural difference, to have somebody on the team that understands what an African American person goes through.… We'd play down south in North Carolina and Duke and places like that. And during that time period, we were called names. We were called devils. Even to the point where 'nigger' or something like that might've come up

Fred Snowden (left) and Johnny Orr outside the "House that Cazzie Built." *BL012412, Bentley Historical Library, University of Michigan.*

a little bit. But it's good to have somebody of your own race that you could talk to about that."

Snowden and Orr also became an excellent recruiting team. But the 1968 recruiting class was complete when Orr became the head coach. Therefore, because freshmen remained ineligible to play on the varsity, Orr coached two full seasons with players recruited to play in Strack's system, except for two junior college transfers.

CHANGING THE TEMPO

Orr made one major change in his first two seasons as head coach: he wanted the Wolverines to run. Orr learned a fast-paced style as a high school player and taught an up-tempo brand of basketball—including aggressive, man-to-man defense—wherever he coached. He hoped to do the same at Michigan, but didn't have all the necessary pieces those first two years. Michigan had played an up-tempo style in the mid-1960s, but Strack's latter teams weren't as quick. "We would've probably been better, to be honest, if Strack stayed," says Orr of his initial two seasons. "Because [the running game] was a different thing for them."

"Orr really wanted us to get that ball up and down the court," adds Tomjanovich. "Strack was more close to the vest, grind it out. But Johnny Orr was, 'Hey, let's get that ball down the court, let's have a very exciting brand of basketball.'"

Orr brought one other distinctive dimension to Michigan basketball. "He was a funny guy," says Tomjanovich. "And he added a lot of fun, just being around him" when Orr was an assistant. "He was still fun when he was a head coach, but with a lot more pressure, and having to win the games, it changes you a little bit. But he was very upbeat, very funny, and I enjoyed just being around him."

C.J. Kupec, who joined the varsity in 1972, says that Orr was "entertaining" and understood the players' point of view. As a result, "You'd run through the proverbial brick wall for Orr because you love playing for the guy."

A pair of complementary players led Orr's first two Michigan squads—the team's scoring and rebounding star, Tomjanovich, plus inspirational leader Dan Fife.

Rudy T was a big forward who was forced to play center on a smaller squad. But he was also an exception on the team because he fit Orr's style more than Strack's. "He was a great shooter and a great rebounder," Orr says. "Oh man, if they'd had 3-point shots he'd have set all kinds of records....If Rudy had come on after I'd been there four or five years I think he'd have been unbelievable. Because Rudy liked to run. And he liked to shoot the ball. I remember him coming to me one time and [telling] me he wasn't getting enough shots. And I said, 'Rudy, you're shooting 30 times a game.' And he wanted the ball more. But he wasn't afraid to take the shot that you needed."

At 6-foot-8, Tomjanovich wasn't a prototypical Big Ten bruiser at center, but he was typical of Orr's post players at U-M. "Rudy liked to shoot and play facing [the basket]," Fife says. "We had nobody, really, who could play with their back to the basket. We lived and died by the jump shot and outrunning people."

Fife, a sophomore on Orr's first squad, was recruited by Strack but didn't care what style the team used—he just wanted to play. And play he did, starting every U-M game during the next three years, while also pitching for the baseball team. As a sophomore, Fife was the team's key surprise as he played a steady game, shot well and inspired teammates with a strong work ethic. "He was a great team player and a real…hard worker," says Orr. "Anything for the team, he would do. He was awesome. He was a leader."

Fife was successful in large part because he accepted Orr's style and understood his role—to play hard, defend the opponent's top-scoring guard and get the ball to Tomjanovich. "I didn't worry about scoring," Fife explains. "Always my thought is, 'If I can do the intangibles I can keep myself in the game.' Then if I got points, that'd only be a bonus."

Fife "would fight for you, and he'd yell at you if you weren't doing well," says Ernest Johnson, who joined the varsity in Fife's senior year. "But he was also the guy that would just talk to you like we were his little brothers. Always cracking jokes. And if you were down and out, he was one of those kind of guys that would come and ask you what's wrong. Just a real good person."

Assists weren't tracked officially when Fife played, but there's no doubt he'd rank among U-M's all-time assist leaders, in part because he frequently—and happily—fed the ball to shooting ace Tomjanovich. "I liked to shoot," Tomjanovich acknowledges. "Probably, looking back at it, and being a young

Rudy Tomjanovich is Michigan's all-time leading rebounder, but he also loved to shoot. *BL009841, Bentley Historical Library, University of Michigan.*

guy, probably way too much tunnel vision at that time. I was just an evolving player, but I do know that I didn't pass up many shots."

Tomjanovich's best offensive day at Michigan was a 48-point effort in an overtime victory over Indiana in January 1969, tying Cazzie Russell's one-game school record. Rudy T hit 21 of 34 shots from the field and went 6-for-8 from the foul line while grabbing 19 rebounds.

Tomjanovich credits his big day, in large part, to Snowden's coaching advice. "He noticed that my shot was flat," Tomjanovich recalls, "so he just recommended that I use the bank shot more....And a week later I scored that 48 points and more than half of 'em were bank shots. I was as surprised as anybody in the arena. It really worked for me. And all those shots that were not comfortable before, all of a sudden became so easy because I'd just get the ball and spin it real hard, snap my wrist and hit a spot on the backboard....My eyes were wide open, like, 'They're all going in!'"

At the same time, he was eager to do the dirty work under both boards. "The one thing that I really think I had over the average player is that I was an offensive rebounder and just an overall rebounder. That was very important to me. That was part of what I thought a good basketball player did. I remember my mother used to say—and she was not a sports fan at all—and she'd just say, 'Why do you always have to be in the middle of all that [physical] stuff? Why can't you be the guy [away from the basket]? Not all those guys run in there and do all that stuff.' But that's what I thought basketball was all about, getting in there, mixing it up and coming up with the ball."

The Wolverines were 13-11 overall, 7-7 in the Big Ten in Orr's first season, and then fell to 10-14, 5-9 in his second. With the excitement of the Cazzie era four years in the past, Michigan's home fans watched the games fairly quietly, unless they were screaming for Orr's head. The anti-Orr crescendo reached a peak when Jim Barahal ran his "Dump Orr" student government campaign in 1973, a tactic he brought directly into Crisler Arena.

"They had signs, when we'd go to the locker room, the kids would drop 'em down when we walked out at Crisler, that said 'Dump Orr.' And they had 'em all over," Orr recalls. "My family couldn't sit together in their seats or anything like that—it was embarrassing. But the guy [Barahal] that started that...later in life he wrote me a heck of a letter and apologized for that."

The few highlights in Orr's second season revolved around Tomjanovich. Early in the year, his 32-point effort helped Michigan beat a strong Marquette squad, 86–78, despite Marquette coach Al McGuire's attempt to distract the U-M star.

"Al McGuire, he's a character," Tomjanovich recalls. Before the game "their starting team, instead of running straight out to the free throw line [during introductions], they ran into the huddle and shook my hand....I said, 'God, they must think I'm pretty damn good if they're going to do that.'... It had the opposite effect of what I think he was trying to do. Because I was so fired up in that game."

In his final college game, Rudy T received standing ovations from the 6,387 fans at the recently christened Crisler Arena when his name was announced at the start of the game and again when he exited, with 41 seconds remaining, just after collecting his 21st and 22nd rebounds of the contest to pass Buntin as Michigan's all-time rebounding leader with 1,039.

Tomjanovich was the second overall pick in the 1970 NBA draft by the then San Diego Rockets that summer and went on to a superlative NBA career as a player and coach. He was inducted into the Naismith Basketball Hall of Fame in 2021.

In 1974, Michigan named its Most Improved Player award in Tomjanovich's honor. Tomjanovich later followed Russell as the second Michigan player to have his jersey honored, in a Crisler Arena ceremony on February 8, 2003, when no. 45 was raised to the rafters.

Orr's Recruits Arrive

Orr's third season, 1970–71, marked a turning point as his first recruiting class joined the varsity. "By the time of my senior year, Orr had [the] kind of player he wanted," Fife says, "getting his kind of kid in, his kid who could play in his system, and believed in him. That's half the battle, trying to get kids to believe in you."

Orr's first recruits stepped in quickly. Sophomores Ken Brady, Ernest Johnson and John Lockard all became three-year varsity contributors. But it was Henry Wilmore, the future All-American, whose fortunes would mirror Michigan's ups and downs over the next three seasons.

Wilmore came from Harlem via Rockwood Academy, a Massachusetts prep school. At 6-foot-3, he was strong and quick and played bigger than his size. Wilmore was an excellent perimeter shooter and was almost impossible to handle man-to-man near the basket, having honed his one-on-one skills on New York's playgrounds. He spent much of his college career with one eye looking toward the NBA, but he remained at U-M for four years and was a hard worker who reportedly never left the court following warm-ups after a missed shot.

"He was an awesome talent," Orr says. "He was as fast with the first two steps as anybody, like a Rickey Green....But he was not the greatest team player in the world, and he was very difficult, sometimes, to play with. [But] when he got the ball, if it was a one-on-one, man-to-man or something like that he could usually beat [his defender]."

"He could handle the ball," Johnson recalls. "He could shoot the jump shot, he could go to the basket, he could pass. He was a leaper. Didn't have a lot of weaknesses to his game. Could play guard, forward. To me I think he was more comfortable playing like the 3, that small forward position, because he could handle the ball so well."

Joe Johnson, who played one season with Wilmore, says that he had two distinct sides to his personality. On the court, Wilmore was more aggressive, with "a unique, sort of a New York style of play that was different than what we were used to in Michigan." Off the court, Johnson notes, "he and I would room together a lot and he was just a very nice person, very reserved, very humble. But just a phenomenal basketball player."

Brady, meanwhile, gave Orr his first and only big, bruising, prototypical Big Ten starting center, a deviation from the Tomjanovich mold of shorter, generally quicker post players. Brady, from Flint Central High School, was 6-foot-11 and weighed about 250 pounds as a sophomore. "First guy I ever saw that could take two basketballs and dunk 'em at the same time, backwards," Ernest Johnson says.

But the key to the team's success that season was getting the ball to Wilmore in a position where he could score. To that end, Orr made team captain Fife a true point guard at a time when few teams employed a single primary ballhandler. Orr then tailored Michigan's offense to suit his primary scoring threat.

Orr's "stack" offense helped free Wilmore from double-teams or tight defenders. When Michigan faced man-to-man defenses, Fife would control the ball, while the second guard, generally Wayne Grabiec, moved to the far side of the court. The other three players often lined up in a stack next to the lane, with Wilmore on top. Wilmore could then move in a variety of directions, depending on how the defense was aligned, and Fife would look to pass him the ball. Against a zone, Michigan often fed Brady in the low post, giving him the option to shoot or to pass to an open man on the perimeter as the zone collapsed around him.

Dan Fife led Johnny Orr's up-tempo offense for three seasons. *BL014066, Bentley Historical Library, University of Michigan.*

Despite the influx of talent, Michigan began the 1970–71 season with losses to no. 6 Notre Dame and no. 5 Kentucky and then was blown out by 21 points at Duke. Fife then helped spark the Wolverines' turnaround during a players-only meeting.

"On Saturday night after the game in Kentucky, I think some guys went out and partied," Fife recalls, "and then we got smoked [by Duke]. I was so mad because we were 0-3, and I knew we were better than that. And I said, 'Guys, I'm telling you, if you do this again—you want to fight me I'll fight you—but I'm telling the coach. You go out and do all this crazy stuff, I'll tell the coaches.'…We went 19-3 after that."

Fife "was a very vocal guy," Ernest Johnson says. "And he was so intense.… He always led by example—diving for loose balls, playing defense. And he stayed on our back. It was almost like he was a second coach in there."

As the season progressed, the Wolverines' fast-break offense began coming together. They went 6-1 following the killer opening week and were playing well together, mainly thanks to the senior leaders. "Brady and Wilmore were so important to our team," Fife explains, "but they knew they had some dues to pay and they respected Rod [Ford] and myself, and pretty much they'd listen to me.…We just had good team chemistry. If you don't, if everybody's not playing for the right reason, no matter what the reason is, you can't win. It's going to destruct."

Back in the Big Ten Race

The Wolverines opened conference play with their first victory in Wisconsin in five years, 90–89, which sparked a U-M winning streak that put the Wolverines in the thick of the Big Ten race for the first time since 1966. Trailing 89–88 with 1:18 left, Michigan held the ball for 1:13 before Grabiec shot from the top of the key. The shot was off target, but when Wisconsin center Glen Richgels swatted the ball away, the officials called goaltending.

"From then on, we won eight straight games in the Big Ten," Fife recalls. "And there's a tremendous difference the way you go and practice [after a victory]….If you lose, no matter how you lose, you're going to practice a different way, in a different mindset. There's people bitching. The issues come out when you lose. The issues keep quiet, most of the time, when you win."

Michigan was the Big Ten's only unbeaten team after winning its first eight conference games, including a key victory over Indiana at home, a 1-point triumph over Northwestern courtesy of two Fife free throws with 59 seconds remaining and four road wins.

Johnson credits Michigan's balanced scoring and an improved up-tempo game for the early conference success. "We got the ball off the glass, and we liked to run," Johnson says. "We pushed it up the court, tried to get layups in transition. We were a pressing team too. We pressed a lot and made turnovers into points."

But Michigan's drive for the conference title went off the rails in a four-day span with losses at Indiana (88–79) and at home to eventual Big Ten champ Ohio State (91–85). The latter game featured Crisler Arena's first-ever sold-out crowd of 13,609 unusually excited fans.

"Every place had crazy fans," Fife says. "Much different than Michigan's. The only time Michigan fans were really loud, I think, was at the Ohio State game.…Everywhere else, you'd go in their crowd and they'd spit on you, just throw stuff at you all the time. It was just rotten. To play in those places and win was just incredible."

But the rare boisterous home crowd didn't inspire the Wolverines in the first half against Ohio State, which rolled to a 20-point lead before Michigan rallied to tie the game at 74 with 6:22 left. The Buckeyes quickly rebuilt their lead to 85–77 before a second Wolverines rally brought them within 87–85 with 46 seconds remaining. With Michigan forced to foul, however, OSU hit four free throws to secure the victory.

"As I look back at it now," Johnson says, "we were playing so well…I kind of remember Fife always saying, 'Don't lose your focus. Don't lose your focus. Yes we are winning…but we can't have any letdowns.' And I think we just kind of peaked out a little bit. Especially us underclassmen, because it's a long season, and it's a lot of games and it's a lot of travel. And I think that it's like we hit a brick wall."

THE FIRST NIT

On the brink of losing any hope of a tournament berth, Michigan won its last four conference games to secure the Big Ten's first bid to the National Invitational Tournament. Previously, the conference champion was the only Big Ten team permitted to join postseason play. "It was very exciting," Orr says. "It was altogether different then, because the NIT really was as big as the NCAA." Indeed, the 1971 NCAA tournament field included just 25 teams, with another 16 invited to the NIT, as compared to the modern 68-team NCAA field.

Nevertheless, the excitement of playing in New York's Madison Square Garden didn't bring out Michigan's best, although the Wolverines did get past Syracuse in the opener, 82–76. U-M was inconsistent, opening leads of 30–17, 43–33 (at halftime) and 63–52, and then allowing Syracuse to rally each time. But Grabiec's perimeter shooting over Syracuse's zone was the key for U-M, as he scored 21 points on 8-for-16 shooting.

Three days later, Georgia Tech ended Michigan's season with a 78–70 quarterfinal victory. The key matchup pitted Brady against 6-foot-10 center Rich Yunkus. Brady finished with a solid 20 points and eight rebounds, but Yunkus scored 27 and grabbed 16 boards.

Michigan ended its season 19-7 overall, 12-2 in the Big Ten, as Wilmore led the way by scoring 25 points per game, the sixth-best one-season scoring average in school history as of 2023. With another talented sophomore class set for the next season, things seemed to be looking up for Michigan and Johnny Orr. But it would take another three years before he found a leader who could replace Fife, who went on to pitch in the major leagues before becoming a successful basketball coach, including a stint as a U-M assistant.

"I'm proud that I played at Michigan but I'm proud to have played for a good team at Michigan" in his senior season, Fife says. "I thought it brought back respect to Michigan basketball. And I thought it really helped Orr get on his way."

A New Crop

The seeds for Michigan's future success were planted a few months before Orr's fourth season, as Orr and Snowden won an in-state recruiting battle for the top-rated high school player in the United States, Campy Russell (no relation to Cazzie) of Pontiac.

"It came down to either going to Michigan or Michigan State," Russell says. "I think, being one of the best high school players in the country and being from Michigan, it was really incumbent on me to go to one of the two schools. I chose Michigan primarily because, when I looked at the two universities—that are both great universities—I just felt like I liked the campus at Ann Arbor. I liked the town, I liked the folks, I liked Johnny Orr, I liked Fred Snowden."

Orr also landed a talented big man from Chicago, C.J. Kupec, and Joe Johnson, a guard from Detroit. That rookie trio would have come in handy immediately—had freshmen been eligible in the 1971–72 season—because Michigan never had its full lineup intact that year. Wilmore missed four late-December games with a knee injury, and Brady sat out the first 14 games following off-season knee surgery. Incredibly, Michigan lost its entire five-player sophomore class during the year due to academic or disciplinary problems.

Eventually, the lineup shuffles resulted in Wilmore's shift to the shooting guard spot, which dovetailed with Wilmore's personal desire to play in the backcourt. Orr confirms that Wilmore wanted to play guard rather than forward because he'd received advice that, at 6-foot-3, he needed to be a guard to eventually succeed in the NBA. Wilmore, quoted in the *Ann Arbor News*, said at the time, "After Coach moved me to guard, I felt much better. Guard is my natural position."

In the short run, Wilmore's move seemed to pay off, as Michigan stood 7-2 in conference play just past the midpoint of the Big Ten season and then beat 8-2 Minnesota before a sold-out Crisler crowd. The Wolverines, despite the veterans' injuries and the sophomores' transgressions, stood alone atop the Big Ten standings at 8-2.

As with the previous year, however, the Wolverines couldn't retain their slim conference lead. They lost three of the final four games—with all three losses on the road—to finish 14-10 overall, 9-5 in conference play, good for third place in the Big Ten. It was disappointing when compared to Michigan's high preseason ranking, but in reality the season marked Orr's most underrated coaching effort, as he kept a team that was devastated by injuries, and thinned by the sophomore class's failures, in competition for conference honors for most of the season.

WHO'S IN CHARGE HERE?

After the season, Strack, the new athletic director at the University of Arizona, hired Snowden as his head basketball coach. Orr replaced Snowden with Jim Dutcher, who'd resigned as Eastern Michigan's head coach in March.

Dutcher was the second of Orr's three lead assistants at U-M. During those twelve years, Orr developed a reputation among some outsiders as being more of a CEO, at best, or at worst a figurehead, rather than a hands-on head coach. The real coach, so they said, was Snowden or Dutcher or, later, Bill Frieder.

But Michigan's players and coaches saw Orr as someone who was confident enough to not only hire excellent assistants but also to delegate them real responsibilities and listen to their advice. "I think Coach Orr was a master in bringing guys in and letting them do what they do and not be a guy who wants to micromanage," Campy Russell says. "I think that was probably his strength....When the game got started, he coached the team. And if [his assistants] had something to say, he let them say it. To me, if you're talking 'Team,' that's what you do. You take the position, 'I don't know everything, so I'm willing to hear what you have to say.' Ultimately, Coach [Orr] made the decisions....To me, the beauty of Coach Orr is that, it wasn't all about him. And I have all the respect in the world for that guy."

Fife recalls a time when he and Frieder spotted an Ohio State offensive tendency during a film session prior to a game. The two assistants devised a strategy to counter the Buckeye tendency and brought the suggestion to Orr. Orr quickly agreed to the plan—even though a *Sports Illustrated* reporter was there observing—which worked well during the subsequent game. "A lot of coaches would've never wanted *Sports Illustrated* to see him in that situation," Fife says, "the two assistants putting this together, and then we go out on the floor and do it. He was comfortable with who he was and wasn't insecure at all with anything."

"I had all great [assistants]. They were all super guys," Orr explains. "I always listened [to them] because they had played for me, or played the system. They were good. And I was an assistant for [four] years, I know how players come to the assistants a lot of times when they've got something on their mind. So I was never worried about hiring great coaches."

Another Russell

Michigan fans had good reason to see the previous year as an aberration and entertain high hopes for the 1972–73 season. After all, Wilmore and Brady were back and healthy, along with fellow seniors Joe Lockard and Ernest Johnson, while the strong 1971 recruiting class—led by Campy Russell, Joe Johnson and C.J. Kupec—was now eligible. Additionally, freshmen were newly eligible to play on the varsity. But it was the sophomore class in general, and Russell in particular, that excited the U-M fans.

Michael Campanella Russell was born in Jackson, Tennessee, but was raised in Pontiac, Michigan. He stood 6-foot-8 and could literally do it all. Technically a forward, he sometimes defended centers or guards. A strong rebounder with good moves in the post, Russell was also an excellent perimeter player and solid ballhandler.

"Campy was just such a natural forward, a natural athlete," Ernest Johnson says. "And we used to like to run. We'd get the ball off the glass. And I remember Campy…he'd say, 'We're the two fastest forwards in the Big Ten, so we've got to get out on the break and run.'…And Campy, he was just such a natural. He could score inside. He had tremendous hands. Hit the perimeter shots."

"Aside from being a great player, he was just one of these unselfish guys," adds Joe Johnson. "If you wanted to borrow Campy's car, you could borrow his car. If you needed his last five dollars, he'd give you his last five dollars. If Campy had a steak and you wanted half, you could have half of Campy's steak. That's the kind of guy he was. And he was the same kind of person on the court.…He just had a good philosophy about basketball. He was the kind of guy [that] if you missed 10 shots he'd say, 'Hey, keep shooting. Don't give up, just keep shooting.' And that was very encouraging to our team."

Joe Johnson was a less-heralded recruit who became a key factor in Michigan's eventual success. Orr offered the 5-foot-10 Johnson a scholarship after viewing Johnson's MVP performance in a high school all-star game. Johnson eventually placed two letters of intent—one from U-M and one from MSU—on a counter in his home and then signed the Michigan tender, in part because "Michigan at that time had a much stronger reputation," Johnson says.

Ernest Johnson calls Joe a "tremendous point guard. Joe was small in stature, but—big heart. I used to love Joe because Joe was one of those point guards that, if you were open he would get the ball to you.…Tremendous ballhandler. Great penetrator. Eventually became a pretty decent shooter."

Campy Russell shoots a jumper in 1974. *BL016935, Bentley Historical Library, University of Michigan.*

Unlike Russell and Joe Johnson, Kupec didn't start during his sophomore year. But he was a regular off the bench—mainly at forward, backing up Ernest Johnson—and saw increased playing time as the season progressed.

A three-sport All-Stater from Illinois, Kupec received a basketball scholarship after choosing Michigan over Notre Dame, but he also played tight end on the football team his first two years in school.

Kupec, Joe Johnson says, "was one of these guys who'd do whatever it took to win. And that's what I appreciated most about him. And off the court, even now, he's always been sort of an encourager. Always kind of keeping everybody together, always encouraging folks to hang in there."

The Russell-led U-M freshman team went undefeated in 12 games in 1971–72. Additionally—and reminiscent of another freshman group from the 1990s—the rookies went head-to-head with the varsity in practice and beat their elders more than once.

Joe Johnson says that the freshman squad "really, really clicked, like early. It was just an incredible sort of meshing of basketball skills. But also personality too. Everybody was very unselfish, and we played together."

Russell says he and his freshman teammates "had real good relationships with each other." He hoped the chemistry would remain when his group merged with the upperclassmen in 1972. He would be disappointed.

Unfortunately for Michigan, Orr believes the veterans who'd battled the freshman phenoms in practice the previous year weren't eager to develop strong bonds with the varsity newcomers, several of whom were about to take some of the veterans' playing time. "The guys didn't get along that well together," Orr says.

With Russell playing forward, Wilmore was now entrenched as a starting guard, although he'd occasionally shift to forward as games progressed. While Wilmore's position was set, the wisdom of his playing guard remained in doubt. Many—including Russell—believed that Wilmore could help the team more by playing small forward, where he could receive the ball on the wing and slash to the basket.

Michigan went 7-3 in the non-conference season, but Orr was constantly adjusting the lineup to get his talented pieces to fit together. Michigan then opened the Big Ten season 4-1 before the clashing parts brought the team down. With chemistry still nowhere in sight, the Wolverines lost seven of their final nine games. In a loss at Iowa, a frustrated Orr drew an unusual technical foul by throwing a towel at a referee to get his attention. "[I] got mad there," Orr recalls. "The clock wasn't working or something. I threw the towel out there at him. I was wild then, my gosh, wild then."

Wilmore averaged 23.6 points per game in his career, good for third on Michigan's all-time scoring list. He, Tomjanovich and Cazzie Russell are the only Wolverines to score 40 or more points in a game three times. But Wilmore didn't realize his ultimate dream and never played a regular-season NBA game.

Orr on Thin Ice?

With Michigan's preseason expectations dashed, the "Dump Orr" movement gained momentum throughout the season. After all, if he couldn't win with Wilmore, Brady and Campy Russell, how could he win?

"Johnny Orr was probably the most likeable guy that you could meet," Ernest Johnson says. "And to see this guy's face, you could see the tension that he had to really go through. He had the pale face. He just looked like he was under a lot of stress. I don't think it affected the way he coached or anything. But I honestly feel bad for him.…He never talked to us about it, but we always, as a team, we used to see those ["Dump Orr"] signs and we would get together as a team and say, 'Let's play hard so that maybe it'll take some of this pressure off Coach Orr.'"

Orr considered resigning after the disappointing year. Canham was also disappointed with the season, but not with Orr. Canham, quoted in the book *Here's Johnny Orr*, said at the time, "John Orr is a good coach, and I'm not going to fire a guy because his team had one bad year."

Canham, Orr recalls, "told me as long as he was there I could be there. He was a great guy, boy. He just wouldn't pay you."

Indeed, Orr was reputed to be one of the lower-paid head basketball coaches in the Big Ten. Like Strack, Orr never had a contract at Michigan. He'd meet Canham every year, haggle over his salary for the next season and then get back to work.

"I remember myself and C.J. going to Coach after that year," Russell says, "and basically I told him, 'Coach, you know, a lot of this wasn't your fault, it was just the fault that we could not come together. But next year, you know, we're going to be very, very good.'"

But even Russell didn't know how good.

LITTLE SKINNY KIDS, 1973–1980

The 1973–74 season marked a turning point for Orr and Michigan. The team was young and small, with the 6-foot-8 Kupec and Russell the only big men. But it was also the first prototypical Johnny Orr squad—fast-breaking, hardworking, tough defensively and, despite the presence of a superstar in Russell, a squad that emphasized team play over individual success.

The '73–74 season was also a milestone for the program, as the eventual architect of Michigan's first NCAA championship team, Bill Frieder, joined the U-M coaching staff.

Unlike most college coaches, Frieder was neither a high school star nor a college player. Instead, he attended U-M's business school and earned an MBA. But as he watched Michigan's powerhouse 1960s basketball teams, his career plans shifted. Rather than go into business, Frieder became a high school teacher and basketball coach. In the '70s, he coached a Flint Northern team, led by Wayman Britt, to a pair of state championships. And when a spot opened on Michigan's coaching staff, Frieder didn't merely apply for the job—he pursued it with the relentless, nonstop determination that would become his trademark. He first approached Orr at a U-M function in Flint. In his autobiography, *Basket Case*, Frieder said that Orr advised him to "stay where you are. I'm gonna get fired anyway." Nevertheless, Frieder followed Orr around for the rest of the day—including a roughly one-hour drive to Saginaw—before Orr agreed to hire him. But the story doesn't end there, as Canham had apparently decided to save money by not filling the vacancy.

So Frieder pursued Canham. When Frieder couldn't get an appointment, he simply sat in the athletic director's office until Canham saw him. The pursuit ended successfully with Frieder's hiring, officially as an assistant coach but mainly as a recruiting specialist.

For two years, Frieder explains, "I was at a lot of the games, but I did mostly recruiting. And then the next five years I was in charge of the recruiting, but other people were out on the road more and I was more John's top assistant, with game preparation. So the seven years as his assistant really prepared me to become a head coach because I had responsibilities in everything."

Campy and Friends Take Charge

The '73–74 team was dominated by the Russell-Kupec-Johnson class. Kupec inherited Brady's post position, and Johnson remained at point guard, while Russell was technically the power forward, although he did everything from scoring to rebounding to ballhandling. "Campy can play forward, guard or center," Orr said before the season. "Too bad I can't have him at all three positions at the same time."

Russell says that Orr's up-tempo style, which allowed Russell to rebound and then bring the ball upcourt himself, fit him well. "So it was just a perfect marriage," Russell adds.

Russell and Kupec were the team's co-captains, with Kupec being the more vocal leader. Additionally, two young leaders helped push Michigan up the Big Ten ladder.

Sophomore Wayman Britt, Frieder's former Flint Northern star, was a preseason contender to start in the backcourt opposite Johnson. But that spot was filled by a surprise candidate: freshman Steve Grote. Grote's emergence created a domino effect that permitted Britt to play forward.

Grote, from Cincinnati, was a two-sport athlete who preferred to play basketball. But as a prep All-American linebacker, college basketball coaches mostly ignored him, assuming that he'd choose the gridiron. In the twenty-first century, he could've drawn multiple basketball offers with just a few words to the right recruiting reporter. But in the early '70s, his preference for basketball remained under the radar.

Indeed, Orr only met with Grote after one of Michigan's football assistants asked Orr to reassure Grote that if he played football at Michigan, he could also play basketball. While Orr was fulfilling his mission, Grote "told me that he wanted to play basketball" full time, Orr says.

Grote had his choice of football offers but received only three major basketball offers, from Michigan, Ohio State and Creighton. Even though Grote was from Ohio, he says that his decision "wasn't close; it was Michigan all the way....I decided that if I wasn't good enough to play professional sports, where did I want to say I had my degree from? And that's where I didn't think it was close—that Michigan was far ahead of a degree from Ohio State."

At most schools, Grote would've been a strong—perhaps even dominant—force, even as a freshman, due to his work ethic and competitive fire. But by choosing Michigan, he found his temperamental equal in Britt. "He and Britt were two fierce competitors," Orr says. "See, now, there's little guys—that team was little, but we out-rebounded almost everyone we played. They were quick, and they could all jump, boy."

The only problem occurred when the pair came too close together at practice. "We couldn't play some of our drills where Britt and Grote were guarding each other because there'd be a fight," Fife says, admiringly. "They literally would fight. So we couldn't run the drills when they were matched up against each other."

Fights aside, Grote says it was "a lot of fun" facing Britt in practice, adding, "You won't find a greater teammate than Wayman Britt because you just know you never had to worry about effort. Yeah, you may not get the breaks, you may not sink the big shot, but you will never get beat because of lack of effort. That's the kind of guy Wayman Britt was, and that's the kind of guys I like to have on my team."

Few coaches would've considered the 6-foot-2 Britt as a potential forward. But Orr, with his emphasis on athleticism, basketball IQ and team play, saw beyond Britt's height. "I'm sure that he wanted to play guard," Kupec says of Britt. "I'm sure he wanted to assume more of a responsibility or more of the load in terms of scoring, because that's the way he did it in high school. But he checked those desires at the door because he was able to see what he could bring to the table" while playing up front.

After an early-season game in 1973, Britt said that playing against bigger forwards was "to my advantage, because I'm faster than they are. I'm OK as long as I box out. I like to win, man. That's all that's on my mind."

During the next four years, Michigan finished no lower than second in the Big Ten. Certainly the Wolverines had talent, including some future NBA stars. But they also won with grit and toughness, epitomized by Britt and Grote. "I think we really played well together," says Johnson, Grote's backcourt mate the next two seasons. "Because we both could handle the ball, we both were great defensive players, we both were real tough. So we

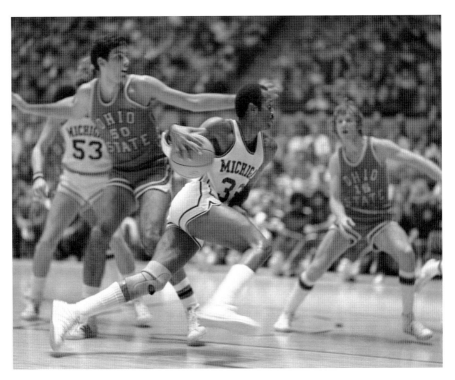

Wayman Britt attacks the Buckeyes. *BL012397, Bentley Historical Library, University of Michigan.*

made it hard on other teams' guards. We shut down a lot of guards because we both were physical."

Orr says he knew Grote would start as a freshman "after about three weeks" of preseason practice. Over the next four years, Grote asserted himself not only with his play but also with his voice. Grote recalls a contest in his junior year when he called a timeout on his own early in the game. "And we went over to the bench, and I just chewed everybody out for the way they were playing because they weren't ready to play—before Coach Orr even said anything. So that was just the natural way I reacted. If people didn't play hard, I got really mad."

With Wilmore's class gone, outsiders had low expectations for Michigan's 1973–74 team. Inside the program, however, the players understood how well their pieces fit. "We just thought we'd be better," Joe Johnson says. "Because we had the nucleus of our [1971–72] freshman team and we knew how we played as freshmen, and we just wanted to get back to that.…We just had a better team philosophy."

Unlike the previous seasons, when the offense featured Wilmore and then Wilmore and Russell, this squad played a team-oriented, pattern offense featuring plenty of movement, with Kupec setting perimeter screens, most often to clear a path for Russell. But Campy was just as interested in setting up his teammates as he was in scoring.

"We had a situation where, going down to the last game of the season, we had a three-way tie for the assist leadership between me, Campy and I think Steve Grote," Johnson recalls. "So we just were very unselfish. I mean, we'd be on a two-on-one break, and I remember, Campy and I, we were both trying to win the assist lead, so I'd give it to him, he'd give it back, I'd give it back. And finally one of us had to shoot. But it was that kind of camaraderie and chemistry that made us a really good team."

Michigan began the season 7-1, but the Wolverines really began turning heads by upsetting a strong, tall San Francisco team—which was destined for the NCAA's Elite Eight—88–66. The reward for U-M's effort was a confrontation with no. 1–ranked UCLA and its 82-game winning streak.

"We played them very, very, very tough," Johnson says. "We pressured them, we pressed them. We were physical with them. And they weren't used to that style of basketball. And we played well, but I think we were a little bit outmanned. But they knew that we competed. And I think that sort of solidified in our minds that it's the type of team we could be."

Michigan beat UCLA's press early—thanks mainly to point guard Johnson—and slowed the Bruins' fast break, taking a 14–8 lead. It was 20–20 a few minutes later, but UCLA was still working hard for every basket. Unfortunately for U-M, Britt was then sidelined with his fourth personal foul. In a mark of how valuable the sophomore was, UCLA promptly went on an 18–6 run and never looked back in a 90–70 victory.

"I think that tournament, actually handling San Francisco, really did a lot for us," Kupec says. "We traveled a long way against a ranked opponent and annihilated them, and then we came back against UCLA and we weren't embarrassed. Not that we were playing not to be embarrassed; we wanted to win the game. But it wasn't a bad performance.…I think overall, though, our non–Big Ten December schedule set the stage for us to do well in the Big Ten."

Jousting with Knight

After facing the no. 1 team in the country, Michigan returned home to meet the consensus Big Ten favorite, eighth-ranked Indiana and its third-year coach, Bob Knight. The Wolverines and Hoosiers would tangle in numerous big games and battle head-to-head for several Big Ten championships during Knight's twenty-nine-year reign in Bloomington. He became a favorite verbal target of the normally reserved Crisler Arena fans, who saw him in his Hoosier-red outfits and just knew that there had to be horns and a tail hidden somewhere underneath. Nevertheless, he and Orr eventually became great friends.

U-M and Indiana had played just twice in the previous two years, with Knight's squad winning both games. But Michigan was ready to turn the rivalry around in the 1974 Big Ten opener.

The game seemed to go according to the expected script as the Hoosiers took a 41–26 halftime lead against a turnover- and foul-prone Michigan squad. But the Wolverines tightened their defense and roared back to take a 61–60 edge with 7:10 remaining.

Michigan maintained its slim lead despite playing the final 3:24 without both Britt and Russell, who fouled out, while Grote and Johnson played on with four personals apiece. Freshman guard Lionel Worrell, subbing for Britt, hit the decisive hoop on a baseline drive to put the Wolverines up 71–69 with 1:07 remaining. Then Grote and Johnson both forced turnovers in the final minute to preserve a 73–71 victory. The victory began a string of five consecutive games all decided by one or two points, of which Michigan won four, including a victory over Michigan State on Kupec's buzzer-beating jumper.

Winning four out of five close Big Ten games "gave us confidence," Johnson says. "We had some clutch players, we had players that weren't afraid to take big shots. And we just were a tough-minded team....When we started winning close games, then we felt like we could win any game."

The Wolverines won their next four contests to take the Big Ten lead at 8-1, one-half game ahead of 7-1 Indiana. But Indiana leapfrogged Michigan with a 93–81 rematch victory in Bloomington, as the Wolverines again battled foul trouble, which exposed their thin bench. With four conference games remaining—including contests against third- and fourth-place Purdue and Michigan State, respectively—Michigan's hopes for a Big Ten title appeared to be fading. But the Wolverines trounced Purdue and edged Wisconsin. Then, while Michigan drubbed Minnesota, the Hoosiers were upset by Ohio State, leaving Michigan and Indiana tied at 11-2.

During Michigan's late bid for the Big Ten championship, "Campy really stepped up," Johnson explains, "and I think that was a big part of what got us over the top. He elevated his performances and we just continued to play tough."

Indeed, Russell scored a career-high 36 points at Wisconsin on February 25 and then matched that total in the regular-season finale at MSU.

The Hoosiers barely clinched their share of the Big Ten crown by edging Purdue, 80–79, while Michigan never let the host Spartans even dream of pulling an upset, rolling to a 15–4 lead on the way to a 103–87 victory, leaving Michigan and Indiana tied at 12-2. Unlike in the mid-1960s, in the 1970s the Big Ten broke first-place ties with a playoff game. So two days after beating the Spartans, Michigan met Indiana on a neutral court at Illinois to determine the Big Ten's lone NCAA tournament representative.

Orr, who preferred man-to-man defense, employed a zone in the first half after missed U-M shots, in part to try to protect his team from fouls, which helped the Wolverines take a 38–36 halftime edge. Grote still ended up with four personals but remained on the court, while Johnson didn't commit a foul. Russell wasn't as lucky, however. After Indiana sliced Michigan's 10-point lead to 4, Russell fouled out with 4:48 remaining. The Hoosiers pulled within 62–61 with 3:27 left, when Orr went to a delay game, successfully stalling Indiana's momentum.

After Kupec scored on a put-back, Grote sank two free throws for a 66–63 lead with 1:31 left. Johnson then pulled a fast one—literally. With Indiana expecting another delay, Johnson zipped past his defender and laid the ball in while drawing a foul from Hoosier center Kent Benson. Johnson completed the 3-point play, opening a 6-point cushion that Michigan never lost in a 75–67 victory.

No Luck for the Irish

Michigan met third-ranked Notre Dame in the NCAA tournament's Mideast Regional semifinal. The Irish, who'd snapped UCLA's 88-game winning streak earlier in the season, entered 25-2 and were favored, but Michigan didn't see itself as an underdog.

"One of the Notre Dame players was quoted as saying, when they saw us going into practice, that we walked in and we carried ourselves as if we knew we were going to win," Grote recalls. "And I just think that was the big strength of that team. We just thought we were going to win."

With Britt dominating at both ends of the court, Michigan almost blew Notre Dame away early. Britt scored 12 points as U-M grabbed an 18–6 lead. The sophomore finished with 18 points and seven rebounds while holding Notre Dame star Adrian Dantley to two points and six boards. "Wayman Britt…almost ran Adrian [Dantley] into hyperventilation," Johnson says.

The Wolverines stretched their lead to 28–8, but the Irish pulled within 34–19 at halftime and then rallied to lead twice in the second half. But Notre Dame couldn't overcome Russell's dominance. Campy scored 18 of 20 Michigan points during one second-half stretch on his way to 36 points and 18 rebounds in a 77–68 victory.

Michigan, now 22-4, then met 23-4 Marquette, ranked seventh in the country. The Wolverines led 39–31 when Al McGuire did all he could to stall Michigan's momentum, taking two technical fouls and calling a timeout after each. McGuire later denied that he'd taken the technicals intentionally. But purposeful or not, his actions helped Marquette pull within 39–37 at halftime.

Michigan maintained a slim edge for most of the second half. U-M led 68–66 with 3:37 remaining, but the Warriors went on a 6–0 run over the next three minutes. After a Russell hoop, Marquette's Lloyd Walton missed a free throw, but Russell missed two long shots from the corner in the final seven seconds, giving the Warriors a 72–70 victory.

"I just remember, as I look back at that game and saw the film later, that I sped my motion up," Russell says of his game-tying attempts. "If you speed your tempo up, you're normally going to miss the shot. But if you stay within your rhythm and your tempo, the chance of you making that shot is greater."

After the season, Orr, who a year earlier had agreed with the majority that believed he'd soon be fired, was named the Big Ten's coach of the year. And the future looked even brighter, as Michigan potentially had all its regulars coming back—until Russell decided to leave for the NBA one year early and was drafted by the Cleveland Cavaliers. "We talk about this all the time," Russell says. "If I would've come back my senior year, I think we'd have probably won the national championship. But at the time I wasn't thinking about that. At the time I was thinking that, 'Hey, you know something, I'm tired of playing college basketball.' I felt like it was just time for me to go."

Replacing Russell

Campy Russell was gone, leaving U-M with one of the great "what ifs" in its basketball history. Had Russell remained, it's conceivable that the 1974–75 Big Ten race could've been a battle between the nation's top two teams: Michigan and an Indiana squad that would lose only once in the next two seasons.

But Russell's absence opened new opportunities for others, most notably sophomore forward Johnny Robinson. A prep star from Chicago, the 6-foot-6 Robinson had hoped to attend U-M with high school teammate Rickey Green in 1973. But Green didn't qualify academically and enrolled in junior college, while Robinson saw action in five games as a U-M freshman.

Robinson "wasn't blessed with great individual offensive talent," Grote says, "but he was a winner. You wanted him on the floor with you because there would be no doubt that he was going to play hard, he was going to do all the right things to bring home a win. He was a very unsung player on those teams." Orr calls Robinson "a steady, solid player. Offense, defense, rebounding. Everything."

Unlike the previous season, when the players had to learn a new offense, the '74–75 team hit the ground running. "We knew the offense much, much better," Johnson says. "We were a little bit more of a pressing team.…And I think we were maybe a little bit better defensively. Campy was more of a perimeter player, but John [Robinson] was more of an inside player. So it allowed C.J. to play outside a bit more and exploit his outside shooting. And John was just a real physical inside presence."

Robinson played off the bench early in the year after turning an ankle, but Michigan still went 7-1 in the pre–Big Ten season. Robinson drew his first start in the conference opener and responded with a 21-point effort in an 86–84 double-overtime victory at Illinois. Michigan suffered through foul trouble and lost Grote and Johnson in the final minutes of regulation, a recipe for disaster the previous season. But freshman David Baxter replaced Johnson and Britt took Grote's guard spot, while sophomore Rick White filled in at forward, and the combination led the Wolverines to a victory. But 10 games into the conference season Michigan was just 5-5, including two losses to Indiana. The Hoosiers, on their way to a perfect conference record, had the title wrapped up.

But there was something new to play for that season. For the first time, two Big Ten squads were now eligible to play in the NCAA tournament, which had expanded to 32 teams. Minnesota and Purdue shared second place at 7-3, while Michigan State was 6-4. Since Michigan would play all three of those rivals at home in the season's final month, a path to postseason play remained open, so Orr called a meeting to try to pump up his team for the stretch run.

"It wasn't a chewing-out session," Kupec recalls, adding, "it was like, we can do better....The attitude came over us—we're just going to work harder than we've ever worked before. I know sometimes people might say, 'Why didn't you have that attitude from the get-go?' Well, you do, but maybe you don't realize you have more in the tank, or you have more resolve than you actually do."

Following the meeting, the Wolverines avenged an earlier loss to Michigan State and then beat Minnesota in overtime as Johnson fed Grote for the winning hoop. After winning two of their next three games, Johnson's 20-footer with two seconds left gave the Wolverines a 77–75 victory over Illinois. On the season's final day, Grote scored 25 to lead U-M past Ohio State in Columbus, 83–64, marking the first time Michigan beat OSU twice in one season since 1947. The victory gave Michigan sole possession of second place in the Big Ten, and U-M was selected for its second straight NCAA tournament appearance.

As an at-large selection in 1975, the 19th-ranked Wolverines traveled to the West Regional to face old nemesis UCLA in Pullman, Washington. The PAC-8 champion and second-ranked Bruins were 23-3 overall and started four future NBA players. But with Johnson slicing through UCLA's press—and Kupec hitting from everywhere, scoring 20 points on 10-for-16 shooting—Michigan led 50–46 at halftime.

"I remember doing a reverse kind of high-off-the-board layup," Kupec says. "I mean, I don't even practice that shot necessarily, but it seemed like the right shot at the right time and it touches the glass and falls in. I mean, everything was going in."

"UCLA of course was not used to our offense," Grote explains, "so we opened up the game [playing well]....I wasn't a very fancy player, but I remember one play there was a missed free throw, and I got the ball and I turned real quickly to start down the floor. And one of their guards was getting ready to come in and take the ball from me. And I actually dribbled behind my back and continued at full speed and hit C.J. for just a classic three-on-one fast break for a layup. And they called timeout, and everybody was hooping and hollering....I remember telling everybody, 'OK, just relax.' Because we had a long way to go in that game."

Coach Johnny Orr loved smaller centers who could play on the perimeter, like C.J. Kupec. *BL013121, Bentley Historical Library, University of Michigan.*

Both defenses tightened up after halftime, as UCLA focused on keeping the ball away from Kupec, holding him to a still-respectable eight points after the break.

Michigan maintained the lead for most of the second half, but with the score tied at 87 and about a minute left, Orr played for the last shot. He eventually wanted the ball in Kupec's hands. Orr got his wish, and Kupec shot from the top of the key with about four seconds remaining. The shot was straight but a hair short, hitting the front of the rim, bouncing up and then away. "We set it up for him to shoot from the free throw line, in the high post," Orr says. "And it worked to perfection, and that was [one of the few] shots he missed all game."

"We worked a sideline out-of-bounds play to perfection for me to come around the 'L' there and to have a little jumper," Kupec recalls, "and when I released it, I always just said, good rotation, felt good. And it just rattled the rim, and instead of rattling a few times and going in, it rattled it a few times and fell out."

When the team returned to the bench after his miss, Kupec adds, "There was a collective sigh of, 'Oh my gosh,' [and] the air just came out of our balloon. And that's a lot of what sport is, is emotion."

As close as the first 40 minutes were, the overtime was lopsided, 16–4 for UCLA over the deflated Wolverines, for a 103–91 victory. "It's very difficult to never be behind in a basketball game and then lose, because we were never behind in regulation," Grote says. Kupec finished with 28 points and brought Michigan to the brink of a tremendous upset. But everyone remembers the final miss.

Kupec recalls attending a home-buying seminar in Ann Arbor a few years later, "and an elderly lady, probably in her sixties or so, she turns and she goes, 'Are you the same C.J. Kupec that missed that shot against UCLA?' And I died, I just laughed. I said, 'Yep,' I said, 'I sure am.'"

UCLA went on to win Coach John Wooden's final national championship, leaving Michigan to wonder: If they could take the eventual champs to overtime without Campy Russell, "What if…?" "You know, we beat UCLA, who's to say what would've happened further on in the tournament," Kupec says, adding that "it's hard not to look at the negatives and say, 'What could have been?' And sometimes you just have to stop and say, 'Hey, but look at all the positives, look at all the successes.'"

Among those successes, Kupec believes that his class, collectively, turned Michigan's program around. "I do believe we saved Johnny Orr's job. I think then it enabled him to recruit great players…and then the stage was set."

Reloading

The Wolverines lost top scorer and rebounder Kupec (who later played with Cazzie Russell and was coached by Rudy Tomjanovich in the NBA), plus lead guard and no. 2 scorer Johnson to graduation in 1975. On the bright side, Johnson's replacement had been waiting in the wings for two years. The new center took longer to locate, but he was worth the wait.

Rickey Green had remained close with his former Hirsch High School teammate Johnny Robinson during the previous two seasons. With Frieder maintaining contact to emphasize Michigan's interest, Green transferred to U-M after his second year in Vincennes Junior College. Green was a late bloomer who began playing organized basketball in seventh grade after discovering his hoops talent accidentally. "I'd never played basketball before, and they had a free throw shooting contest at the park that I was at," Green recalls. "And I ended up winning it."

Meanwhile, Orr and Frieder knew who they wanted to replace Kupec, but they didn't know until about three months before the 1975–76 school year whether they'd get him. But they did know that chief recruiter Frieder would either sign his target or kill his car trying.

Frieder recalls that in the first half of 1975, "I was home for dinner less than five days." He either ate on the road or in Canton, Ohio, in pursuit of McKinley High big man Phil Hubbard.

Hubbard was Ohio's high school player of the year in 1974–75. He grew up an Ohio State fan and had "major interest" in playing for the Buckeyes. In the end, Hubbard also considered Iowa, Iowa State and Pittsburgh, along with Michigan. But he was one of many high school stars to receive the all-out Frieder recruiting onslaught.

Frieder, who was sometimes accompanied by Campy Russell, then playing for the Cavaliers, attended Hubbard's games and practices religiously. His approach "was aggressive and it was consistent and it was very persistent, too," Hubbard recalls. "He was a never-let-up guy. He was always there."

Nevertheless, Hubbard's recruitment dragged on until June, when he finally signed with Michigan. The 6-foot-7 Hubbard played center in high school. However, "I thought that I'd be playing forward; no more center in college," Hubbard recalls. "I wasn't quite that big. But it just happened that they had two decent forwards—Wayman Britt and John Robinson—and they were returning lettermen. And the only spot open at that time happened to be center."

To Orr, however, Hubbard was "definitely a center. He was only 6-7, but strong, good jumper, great timing, and a super, super, guy."

"I just couldn't believe how smart, mature and confident he was as a freshman," Grote recalls. "Because he's coming in and joining a program that was very successful and had been completely turned around. And I mean from day one, when he stepped on the floor, it was very clear, he expected to be a starter and he expected to win when we played."

Indeed, Hubbard "expected, wherever I went, I was going to play," he says. "It didn't matter. There was no doubt in my mind. Michigan, Ohio State, any of those schools on that list, I was starting."

His new teammate, Green, wasn't quite as confident. "I did not expect to start, but I knew that I could hang with the guys that were there," Green says. "I didn't see anyone that was that much better than me."

Whatever his expectations, Green established his presence during informal, preseason scrimmages with his established U-M teammates. "We had some throw-down games....It was more so like, staking your ground, that's how I looked at it," Green explains. "I had to come in there and show them that I was ready to play at that level."

Once practice began, the coaches knew they'd found replacements for Kupec and Johnson. "Rickey Green, the first day of practice you knew he was a player," Frieder says. "There was no one who accelerated the ball quicker than he did. He seemed to be faster with the ball than without the ball. And Phil Hubbard you knew was a player. And obviously until it all meshes together you don't know. But we knew we had good talent."

With Hubbard and Green filling the open center and guard spots, "We ended up with the same type of team," Grote says. "So Rickey Green, very similar-type player to Joe Johnson. And then Phil, of course, was a better offensive player than C.J., just because he was faster and quicker.... Because of Phil Hubbard's better athletic ability, you probably had a slight pickup in talent."

That talent didn't end with Green and Hubbard, although the duo instantly became Michigan's top two scorers. Indeed, U-M had so much talent that heralded prep stars Alan Hardy and Tom Staton saw little action in the regular season, although Staton played a key role in Michigan's NCAA tournament run. Staton says that the Wolverines "weren't big, we weren't tall. We were, as Johnny Orr called it, his bunch of little skinny kids. But we had speed, heart, desire and the ability to shut people down."

Michigan finished 6-2 in non-conference play—including a 1-point loss at top-10 Tennessee—a promising showing for a revamped team. "There was

Rickey Green out-leaps Iowa. *BL012384, Bentley Historical Library, University of Michigan.*

a good mixture of young and old guys and new guys that came together," Hubbard says. "As the season went on, we got stronger and more confident in our playing together."

This was the quintessential Johnny Orr team, the squad that proved his point that athletes could succeed on the court no matter their height.

Hubbard, the undersized center playing in perhaps the most physical conference in the nation, averaged 11 and 13 rebounds per game, respectively, in his first two seasons. Robinson, also small for a power forward, more than held his own at both ends of the floor, while Britt, the very undersized small forward, continued to negate taller opponents with his quickness, leaping ability, smart play and pure grit.

"One of the keys to our team was Wayman Britt," Frieder says. "Because at 6-foot-2 he was good enough to guard a 6-7, 6-8 guy, keep 'em off the boards. And once we got the ball—because he had the quickness and speed of a guard—we always got fast break advantages because we were quicker down the court."

But for all the Wolverines' talent, it was Green's speed that set them apart. "You could throw the ball to him, on the outlet, and in three dribbles he was at the opposite foul line, taking off with that patented spin/finger roll," Staton says.

While his speed turned heads in Vincennes, Green says he didn't reach peak velocity until he entered Orr's conditioning program. "I never ran as hard in my life in practice as I did at Michigan," Green says. "And I think that we were so much in better condition than other teams, that made us stand out more so than anything."

With Hubbard and Green blending into the lineup seamlessly, and a deep bench available when needed, Orr was pushing the right buttons. But Staton notes that Orr was also smart enough to know when not to push any buttons. "One time down at Ohio State, we were down by 10 with about three minutes to go," Staton recalls. "And finally Coach Orr called a timeout, and he comes over and he says, 'OK guys, just go out there and get some rebounds and win the game.' And literally, that's what we did….Most of the times we were better with less coaching because athleticism just would take over."

Tipped by the Hoosiers

Michigan breezed through its first three conference games before the initial showdown with Indiana. A record 14,063 fans squeezed into Crisler, but they were quickly disappointed as the Hoosiers rolled to a 16–2 lead on the way to an 80–74 victory. Hubbard drew four early fouls and then played well into the second half before fouling out with a team-leading 23 points. But Indiana center Kent Benson more than countered with 33 points on 16-for-18 shooting.

"I remember Benson never fouling out against Michigan, and I always felt he had seven, eight fouls against us," Frieder says. "I guess give credit to Knight to teach him how to foul without getting caught."

The disappointed Wolverines won their next three games before suffering a 76–75 upset at Illinois that featured an odd, frustrating ending. U-M missed three shots on its final possession before a Robinson put-back fell through the hoop at the buzzer, but the apparent basket was waved off by the officials. At that time, a last-second "uncontrolled shot"—such as a missed shot that was tipped back into the basket—would only count if the ball passed completely through the hoop before the buzzer sounded. In the case of Robinson's put-back against Illinois, the referee ruled that the ball was still on the rim when the clock hit zero, which gave the Illini the victory.

The Illinois wake-up call led to two solid victories before the Wolverines, 8-2 in conference play, traveled to Bloomington to face the still-unbeaten Hoosiers, who were 9-0 in the Big Ten. "At that time, Assembly Hall was one of the most difficult places to play," Staton says. "They had 17,000 students who looked like they were just lined up, up a wall, yelling down upon you. You couldn't hear yourself think, much less call out a play. And with their pressure defense, it was truly, truly a difficult environment to win."

But this time, Michigan gained the early advantage, harassing Indiana with multiple defenses and taking a 39–29 halftime lead. Indiana never led in regulation time but pulled within two points in the last minute. In the final seconds, Indiana missed two shots before Benson tipped the ball up. The ball was in the air as the buzzer sounded and then dropped through the hoop— seemingly the same situation as Robinson's disallowed basket at Illinois, as replays clearly showed Benson tipping the ball with one hand. But Benson's basket counted, sending the game into overtime at 60–60.

"When Benson tipped that ball up and it hit the board," Grote says, "I immediately went to the officials because I would bet that they didn't know the rule—because it's a stupid rule, why would you even know it? I said, 'No that was not a basket.'…I said, 'An uncontrolled shot had to be through the basket, and that was a tip.' So you know what they told me they ruled? 'It was a controlled tip.'"

Looking back three decades later, Orr says, "If it'd been in Ann Arbor, we'd have won that game."

Michigan shook off any disappointment and took a 64–60 lead in OT but couldn't hold on. Scott May's jumper gave the Hoosiers their first lead of the day, 68–67, with 1:26 left. Michigan never scored again and fell, 72–67.

Asked about Benson's tying basket after the game, Orr noted that "at Illinois we tipped the ball in like that, and the referee said we didn't have control and we lost. Today, the ref said he had control of it. What can you say? It looked like an identical thing to me, but we lost both games."

Indiana was now clearly in the Big Ten's driver's seat. But as with the previous season, Michigan could expect an NCAA berth by placing second in the conference. Unlike the year before, the runner-up spot wasn't in doubt, especially after another U-M victory over third-place Purdue. Michigan won six of its last seven Big Ten games to enter the NCAA tournament 21-6.

Tournament Tom Shocks Wichita

Unlike previous years, the ninth-ranked Wolverines weren't sneaking up on anybody in NCAA play. They were the clear favorite in their Midwest Regional opener in Denton, Texas, against Missouri Valley Conference champion Wichita State. But the Wheatshockers started fast and remained on top, leading 60–48 with 11:17 left. Then Orr made the unlikely move that probably saved Michigan's tournament run.

Tom Staton recalls sitting on the bench—and expecting to remain there—when "all of the sudden I hear somebody say, 'Staton!' And I'm looking around in the stands, 'Who's calling me?' And Dave [Baxter] says, 'Tom! Coach wants you, Coach wants you!' So I look down and I'm reaching for a towel, I'm thinking he wants a towel, you know Johnny and Bill were famous with their towels, right?…So I'm reaching for a towel, and Orr looks and says, 'Staton! Get down here!' And I'm running down there, and he says, 'Take your [warm-ups] off, you're going in!' And I'm probably the most shocked person in the entire arena. So I go in, and he says, 'Go in, get us going out there.'

"I go in, Rickey Green throws me the ball, I throw it back to him—I definitely didn't want to make a mistake. He throws it back to me. So I turned and I looked and I took a dribble, and I pulled up [and shot] from about 23 feet—and of course I was scared to death that it was going to miss, so I ran underneath, expecting to try to get a rebound, right? And it splashed straight through, bam! So, wow, I'm so happy. I turned and act like I'm happy that, hey, I'm a freshman and I scored. And I act like I'm running back, and they turn and throw the ball in and I sneak back and swipe the ball and put it up for another layup."

Staton's two hoops in seventeen seconds reduced Wichita's margin to eight. The Wolverines were back in the game and soon took a brief lead, but they slipped behind, 73–72, in the final minute. With Wichita in possession, Grote took one for the team, or at least acted the part. "I faked a charge," Grote says. "And I couldn't believe I got the call, but the other guy went up in the air to make a pass and so I started falling as soon as I could."

Hubbard had fouled out, so Green was the likely candidate to take the last shot, even though he was only 3-for-16 from the floor to that point. "We were going to set him up to shoot the shot because they had a tough time guarding him," Orr says, "and he could get open."

Indeed, Green came open off a screen, got the ball in the corner with six seconds remaining and drained the winning hoop in a 74–73 victory. "When they went up by one they were laughing and clapping and saying they thought they had the game won," Green says. "And I do remember hitting that shot and seeing their faces, their heads going down."

In addition to drawing the key charge, Grote led Michigan with 17 points. But Grote and Green's heroics wouldn't have been possible without U-M's bench play, particularly Staton's.

Staton was a highly recruited prospect out of Ferndale, Michigan, another player who was pursued relentlessly by Frieder. Otherwise, Staton might've been on the other side of the Michigan-Indiana rivalry. But Staton recalls that Knight didn't impress his parents when the Indiana coach paid a recruiting visit to Staton's home. "My dad was also a pastor, and so Bobby Knight came in with his, 'Goddamn we just…' He came in with that foul mouth, and after he left my mom…looked at me and said, 'You don't want to go play there, do you?'"

Now, after coming seemingly out of nowhere to help Michigan survive its NCAA opener, Staton was dubbed "Tournament Tom" in the press. By Staton's recollection, however, his performance saved more than just Michigan's future. "Johnny Orr, a couple games later, he says, 'Ha-ha Staton, you've got a great run here, man. Great job, great job.' He says, 'But, ha-ha, partner, I'm just letting you know, if you had missed that first shot [against Wichita], you'd have never played at Michigan again.'"

After edging Wichita State, Michigan traveled to Louisville to face seventh-ranked Notre Dame. The Irish seniors, including Adrian Dantley, were looking to avenge Notre Dame's tournament loss from 1974. It would be up to Britt, now assisted by Staton, to slow Dantley, who was averaging 28.5 points per game.

Dantley managed 31 points this time, but Michigan beat him with teamwork, as five Wolverines scored in double digits, led by Rickey Green with 20. The Irish led by as many as 11 points in the first half, but a 16–4 run helped U-M pull within 41–40 at the break. Green, who'd bruised a thigh in practice, played with his leg taped heavily—too heavily, apparently. He scored just four points in the first half but removed the wrap shortly before halftime, and his play picked up.

It was 60–60 with 8:46 left in the second half when Britt fouled out, leaving Tournament Tom to face the dangerous Dantley. Staton held his own and then made his biggest play of the game with 2:37 left, intercepting Dantley's inbounds pass and driving for a layup. Grote scored what proved to be the decisive points with 27 seconds remaining when he canned both ends of a 1-and-1 for a 78–74 lead in an eventual 80–76 Michigan victory.

U-M then battled Big Eight champion Missouri for the regional crown. The Tigers were a tough defensive team that entered the game 26-4. Nevertheless, they seemed a lesser opponent when compared to Notre Dame. And Michigan treated them as such in the first half, racing to a 10-point lead four minutes into the contest and increasing the margin to 41–23 at halftime.

At the break, Orr reminded his troops that the number to remember was 20—the minutes remaining in the game—rather than 18, Michigan's lead. Despite that reminder, Missouri rallied and tied the game at 65 with 12 minutes left, thanks mainly to guard Willie Smith, who scored 29 of Missouri's 51 second-half points.

The score was 71-all when Smith sank a pair of jumpers and a free throw for a 76–71 lead with 7:54 left. That run finally roused the Wolverines, who pulled back to 77–77 with 6:14 on the clock. After a Smith free throw, Robinson put U-M on top to stay by sinking two free tosses. Missouri couldn't rally again, and Michigan was a 95–88 winner.

As the regional champion, Orr recalls, "We felt we were getting better and better, winning those close games. We joked about it, 'Let's not be so close next time,' and stuff like that to kind of loosen us up. But they felt confident and so did I….We really played up to our abilities, and beyond, in the NCAA tournament."

Making History in Philadelphia

Michigan returned to the Final Four—played at Philadelphia's Spectrum— for the first time in eleven years and, says Grote, "didn't know anything" about their next opponent, unbeaten Rutgers. "But that didn't matter…. We were going to play our game; you better be ready for us, and that's kind of the way things were. We went in there to the Spectrum for our pregame practice before the Rutgers game, and I'm telling you we stunk it up…we just had a terrible, terrible practice. And then came out [in the game] and we destroyed 'em."

The Scarlet Knights seemed a mirror image of the Wolverines. A small and quick squad that pressed constantly, Rutgers entered the game ranked fourth and sported a shiny 31-0 record, although it included just two victories over ranked teams. "We were happy we got them because they were runners and so were we," Orr says. "Only they were 31-0. But we felt good, and [with] the scouting reports and everything, we felt strong. If we played our game, we could beat them. They weren't as powerful as the teams that we'd played getting there."

The game was close for just more than 10 minutes. U-M then went on a 9–0 run for a 26–14 lead. The shocked Knights, who'd never trailed by more than seven points all season, couldn't handle the deficit. Nor could they stop Michigan's ballhandlers, who repeatedly shattered Rutgers' press on the way to easy layups. The Wolverines carried a 46–29 lead into halftime and, unlike the Missouri game, never let up. Their second half lead meandered between 15 and 23 points before settling at 16 in an 86–70 victory.

Meanwhile, Indiana won the other semifinal, making the 1976 final the first NCAA basketball championship game played by two teams from the same conference. Arguably, however, 31-0 Indiana was in a league of its own.

Asked after the Rutgers contest if Michigan had just played its best game, Orr didn't hesitate. "Oh, no. We lost that one," he said, referring to the game at Indiana. Orr's comment put in blunt perspective just how good Indiana was, while highlighting the fact that Michigan did need to play its best game of the season to stay with the Hoosiers.

Michigan and Indiana might've been from the same conference, but Staton says the teams were temperamentally different. "We remember pulling up to the Spectrum [for] the Indiana game," Staton says, "and all the Indiana guys getting off the bus in their red jackets, we called them the 'Automatons,' the robots, all of them looking alike, with the same haircuts and everything….Then you looked at our team getting off the bus, we were the equivalent of the NBA and the players today. We were the forerunners, we were the ones getting off the bus in the blue jean bellbottoms with the Gucci names on 'em and the T-shirts and the leather jackets and the hats cocked to the side."

Assistant coach Fife, meanwhile, was impressed with the players' demeanor. "They never seemed to get like they were nervous about where they were at or the surroundings," Fife recalls. "It was just, get out on the floor and start competing. I was always amazed at that."

"We weren't intimidated by 'em," Orr says. "But we knew we had to play awfully well, and we had to do a lot of things that we didn't have to do against other teams because of Benson and Scotty May. And they were a great basketball team."

Michigan played its game to near perfection in the first half, defending and rebounding well and running the break effectively. Additionally, with the score tied 4–4 in the opening minutes, Indiana guard Bobby Wilkerson suffered a concussion when he tried to take a charge against Britt. Wilkerson would be OK, but his night was done. Indiana had lost its floor leader.

Michigan continued to run the break successfully. Robinson outletted to a surging Green for a basket and a 12–8 Michigan lead. After a Quinn Buckner hoop, Hubbard scored on a drive, Britt hit from the left corner and Grote nailed a jumper for an 18–10 U-M lead after eight minutes.

After a timeout, a 9–0 run put the Hoosiers up by a point. But in the closing minutes of the half, Britt set up Robinson for a fast break hoop, and then Green was fouled on another break and sank two free throws to give Michigan a 35–29 halftime lead.

In the first 20 minutes, Michigan out-rebounded Indiana and shot 61.5 percent from the floor. The Wolverines scored 12 points directly off the break, plus Green's two free throws after he was fouled on the run. Michigan had been called for just six fouls, and Indiana had only hit one free throw. But in the U-M locker room, Frieder was worried. "I remember telling Johnny Orr at halftime…'Coach, we're playing as well as we can possibly play, and that's a concern. Can we keep this kind of play up, and will Indiana take it up a notch?'"

Grote, meanwhile, recalls that "I was more exhausted at halftime of that game than I had ever been at the end of a game. We went in there at halftime, and I mean I just remember lying on the training table and I was just exhausted. And you know what was funny? I never saw a replay of that game until [2009], and so, as I was watching it, you did notice that Indiana was substituting; we were not, and so I think that did catch up to us."

Indeed, Michigan's only first-half sub was Tom Bergen, who spelled Hubbard in the final minute. Another key factor was the play of Wilkerson's eventual replacement. After trying two others, Knight inserted Jim Wisman at point guard late in the first half. Wisman played a pass-first style, and in the second half he directed Indiana's offense efficiently. He ended up leading Indiana with six assists while committing just one turnover in 21 minutes.

In retrospect, Orr says, "The big thing that hurt us in that game, more than anything else, [Wilkerson] got hurt, their great player. And they brought [Wisman] in, and he got the ball to Scotty May and to Benson and [Quinn Buckner], who was a great guard. And [Wisman], all he did was kind of direct the traffic for 'em and do everything. Actually, it turned out, they lost a great player in [Wilkerson]—not saying that we'd have beaten them had he been there, but I think it would've been a different type of game."

While Michigan dictated the play in the first half with its quickness, Indiana dominated the second half with power, precision and strong defense. The Hoosiers set the tone immediately, as Benson scored on a put-back, and then May was fouled grabbing an offensive board and sank two free throws. Then the fouls began piling up. Britt drew his fourth and went to the bench with U-M on top, 39–35.

The Wolverines enjoyed two more brief leads, but a pair of Benson jumpers helped Indiana take a 47–43 edge, and the Hoosiers never trailed again. Michigan did tie the game at 51 midway through the second half, but Indiana responded with five straight points, while Hubbard drew his fourth foul. Shortly thereafter, Hubbard fouled out battling for an offensive board, with 7:27 remaining. Still, Michigan hung in the game, as Grote sank four straight free throws to pull the Wolverines within 63–59 with about six minutes left. Indiana then broke the game open with a quick 8–0 run, while Britt drew his fifth personal. From that point on, Indiana played keep-away while Michigan went into all-out desperation mode, leading to more free throws and some easy Indiana buckets as the Hoosiers completed their unbeaten season with an 86–68 victory.

"It actually was a much closer game than it was [on the scoreboard]," Staton says. "We just went out like warriors, instead of trying to keep it close.…We not only had a chance to win, we really felt that we should've won."

"We always thought we could beat Indiana," Green recalls, "because we played 'em so close and so tough. And when Bobby Wilkerson went out, we felt that we had a good shot to win. A few calls here or there could've kept us in the game. I've watched the game a few times, and looking at some of the calls, I'm like, 'Man, how could he call that?' A couple of breaks here and there, I think we would've been right there, if Phil didn't foul out."

Michigan finished 25-7, setting a single-season school victory record (although the mark only stood for one year). Additionally, the one consolation from the springtime loss was the knowledge of what lay ahead in the fall, as Michigan returned four starters, while Indiana was losing four.

"We were really, really good" the previous three seasons, Grote says. "We got unlucky to be really good when what I believe is the best college basketball team ever was in our league."

No Britt, but Plenty of Grit

The fall of 1976 marked one of the most confident periods in Michigan basketball history. After all, just one player—albeit a good one—graduated from the team that reached the NCAA pinnacle, and a ready replacement seemed at hand in Michigan's 1976 tournament sparkplug, Tom Staton.

"That was Johnny Orr's style, having the small forward, or what we know now as the three-guard front," Staton explains. "For about 10 years there [Michigan] had a premier, either offensively or defensively, small forward," meaning Wilmore and then Britt and then Staton. "I was kind of heir apparent because of the way they wanted to run and because of my ability to rebound and get up and down the floor."

Staton's strategy for guarding bigger forwards was to "deny them the ball, beat them to the spot, use my strength against them, use my quickness."

Michigan also remained small at center. During the previous season, Orr and Frieder had aggressively but unsuccessfully tried to recruit some premier post players, hoping to then move Hubbard to forward. Looking back, Hubbard notes that his opponents "might've been a little stronger than me. But I just went and played my game and worked hard and just did what I could. But I never really looked at it as, I was going to play this guy, and this guy was big. I never even thought about it like that. I just thought about it like, 'Hey, we got a game, that's my man, I'm going to play him and I'm going to see what happens.'"

Orr says Hubbard handled bigger centers "very well. And what he could do, he could bring 'em outside. He could shoot that free-throw [line] jump shot. He could really hit that shot…[and] he had a very quick first step. If those big guys came out there on him, he'd go right by 'em. And he was a real cog in the thing. He was probably the main man."

"We had the smallest but most exciting, quickest, high-scoring team in the country," Staton says. "And nobody liked to play us. Because we backed down from no one."

Orr says that Michigan's talent was so good, "we didn't prepare as much for the other team; we prepared for ourselves, what we did. And we felt if

Michigan center Phil Hubbard battles Indiana nemesis Kent Benson. *BL012393, Bentley Historical Library, University of Michigan.*

we played our game, got them playing the way we wanted to play, we could either beat 'em, or it would be a very close game."

Michigan's 1976 tournament run also inspired fans to fill Crisler Arena. And the fans were loud enough to finally give U-M a strong home court advantage. "That was a great benefit because…we were winning and people started really coming to the games," Orr recalls. "And the students got into it a little more. Crisler was a great place to play. You didn't have a track in there. The fans were right down on the floor. And it was very noisy. The band was terrific."

As the season began, U-M was ranked first in the AP poll and second in the UPI, although Michigan was soon ranked no. 1 in both polls. Michigan's pre-conference schedule—which contained no ranked teams—was uneventful, except for a late-December tournament in Rhode Island where the Wolverines suffered a stunning 82–81 double-overtime upset against host Providence College.

Michigan entered the Big Ten season 7-1 overall and, despite the Providence upset, was still ranked third and fifth in the two polls. The favored Wolverines entered the conference campaign "with a target on our backs," Staton says, particularly on the road.

"In Minnesota they poured beer on you, back in those days, when you came out of the locker room," Staton recalls. "It was frightening sometimes. Indiana was frightening, being in that gym, with Bobby Knight slapping his players and throwing chairs. Michigan State with their scoundrels on the sidelines, talking to you all the time, from beginning to end, was just a horrible place to play in the old gym, where they were right up on top of you in the old IM building. Ohio State in the barn was just awful to play in because once they started stomping in that old wooden barn it felt like that 20,000 was going to come right through the balcony and fall right on top of you."

Michigan began the Big Ten campaign with a bigger look, with 6-foot-8 junior Joel Thompson starting at center and Staton playing off the bench. Orr made the change following the Providence loss, in anticipation of facing some zone defenses, and in the hope that Staton would provide a spark off the bench, as he had in the NCAA tournament.

The Wolverines opened 8-0 in Big Ten play and then stumbled at Northwestern, a team they'd beaten by 37 points a few weeks earlier, 99–87. Michigan then gutted out its first victory over Indiana in six tries. The teams were tied at 79 with 2:07 remaining, but U-M sank 10 straight free throws for an 89–84 victory. Green finished with 32 points, while Staton replaced Thompson in the starting five, as Orr said Staton provided the best matchup against Indiana's starters. But Staton remained a starter for the rest of the season.

After drilling Ohio State, 10-1 Michigan traveled to 7-1 Minnesota—coached by former Orr assistant Jim Dutcher—where Grote's baseline jumper broke an 80-all tie in an 86–80 U-M victory. After losing at Indiana, Michigan regained the Big Ten's driver's seat with an impressive victory over Iowa, followed by an 89–70 beat-down of Minnesota.

Michigan clinched a tie for the conference crown by winning at Illinois but lost Green with a bruised right hip. With Baxter contributing 20 points and 10 assists in Green's spot and Hubbard scoring a career-best 31 points, Michigan then earned the undisputed Big Ten title with an 84–79 victory at Purdue to finish 16-2 in conference play.

The next day, Green spent just two minutes on the floor in his final home game as Michigan edged 19th-ranked Marquette, 69–68. Grote scored just two points in his Crisler send-off, but they were the clinching free throws with 23 seconds remaining. Had matters gone differently in the NCAA tournament, the teams could've played a rematch in the Final Four. As it was, both national polls reinstated Michigan as the nation's no. 1 team following the victory.

Dueling with Dickie V

Michigan entered NCAA play in the Mideast Regional slot reserved for the Big Ten champion, in the final year before the tournament began seeding its contestants. Those who believed in omens didn't appreciate where the Wolverines had to begin—Assembly Hall in Indiana—although the team found good-luck wishes from Knight upon its arrival to face Holy Cross.

The 23-5 Crusaders, a major underdog, gambled by crashing the offensive boards hard. The tactic was successful for a while; only an 11-for-13 shooting spree by Green kept Michigan within 40–39 at halftime.

But Holy Cross's offensive strategy left the Crusaders open to fast-break counterattacks. Leading 72–70 with a little more than five minutes remaining, Michigan scored eight straight points in a 1:40 span, as Baxter set up Bergen for a basket and scored three hoops himself for an 80–70 lead with 3:30 left.

With Green scoring a career-best 35 points on 16-for-20 shooting, plus nine assists, Michigan topped Holy Cross, 92–81. "Holy Cross played all right; everybody was up for it," Hubbard recalls. "But the big game was going to be Detroit."

The University of Detroit reached its peak under Coach (and later TV star) Dick Vitale in 1977. With future NBA performers John Long, Terry Tyler and Terry Duerod, the Titans compiled a 26-2 mark, including victories over then top-10 teams Marquette and Arizona. Moreover, Vitale constantly goaded Michigan about its refusal to play U-D. Michigan had last scheduled the nearby Titans in 1973.

"Detroit was pretty good at that time," Hubbard says. "They had good players, and they always kept telling us that we should play them. And Dick Vitale kept saying that, not the players. I actually went to Frieder one time and said, 'Why don't we play Detroit?' And he said, 'No way.' He said, 'It's not going to happen. We have nothing to gain....' So it just worked out that we played them in the tournament. We knew we'd be ready because Dick Vitale always talked about stuff, that we were ducking him. The coaches may have been ducking them, but the players never did."

After U-D clobbered Middle Tennessee State in the first round, Vitale received his dream matchup against Michigan in Lexington, Kentucky. In the opening minutes, however, it probably seemed more like a nightmare to Vitale, as a 16–2 Michigan run gave the Wolverines an 18–8 lead. But U-D chipped away and was down just 48–44 at halftime. Michigan increased its advantage to eight before another Titans rally knotted the contest at 66 with 8:52 left. The explosive Wolverines then pulled away for good with a 7–0 run in the next 47 seconds, rolling to an 86–81 win.

Michigan won the game on the glass, out-rebounding U-D 51–33, led by Hubbard's career-best 26 boards. Later, however, Vitale would claim that the Titans took so much out of Michigan that the Wolverines couldn't refocus in time to win the regional final. Frieder partially agrees.

"He had great talent, Detroit did, and it was a great game," Frieder says. "I think the game probably cost us the next game....I think there was so much hype on [the U-D] game, I do think it led to a letdown on our part."

That "next game" involved the University of North Carolina–Charlotte and is one of the most disappointing in U-M basketball history because it cost the nation's top-ranked team a shot at a national championship. The 49ers were ranked just 18th, but the Sun Belt Conference champs were 27-3 and reached the regional final by destroying Syracuse, 81–59.

"We thought we were going to win," Green recalls, "because we were there [in the Final Four] last year. I thought we were going to make it to the finals. I don't know if I would say I was overconfident, but I thought we would beat them because they were a smaller school."

"They were really, really good, and no one knew anything about them," Grote says. "We didn't. Back then you didn't really know that much about the other teams because [few] games [were] on TV."

UNC's strategy was to take away Michigan's inside game. The 49ers played a combination 2-3 zone but kept a man on Hubbard, who shot just 1-for-7 in the opening half and 5-for-14 for the game. Michigan couldn't shoot Charlotte out of the zone in the first half and wasn't getting its characteristic load of offensive rebounds, allowing the 49ers to take a 40–27 halftime lead.

The Wolverines caught up in the second half, turning up the defensive pressure, forcing turnovers and gaining some easy hoops to take a 49–48 edge with 12 minutes remaining. To counter the Wolverines' press, Charlotte coach Lee Rose then had the 6-foot-8 Cedric "Cornbread" Maxwell, the future Boston Celtics star, advance the ball over midcourt. A deft ballhandler, Maxwell broke the press consistently and also caused Staton to foul out.

"Down the stretch, it was unbelievable when we knew the only way we were going to win is we had to steal the ball," Grote recalls, "and they started letting Cornbread Maxwell bring the ball up the floor, and he was guarded by Tommy Staton. Tommy Staton was 6-foot-4, great quickness and outstanding defender, and he couldn't take the ball from him."

With a 1-point lead and 12 minutes remaining, Staton believes that Michigan was "getting ready to cruise right on out as we usually would." However, "in the next 2:11 of game time the same referee called three fouls on me and two fouls on Steve Grote and fouls us both out of the game….And the other referee was like, 'I don't know what he's calling.' After that, Cornbread Maxwell—who was a mismatch of course, as he was one of the great NBA players himself because of his ability to handle the ball at 6-8—he just handled the ball, took it over and took our regional championship away from us almost single-handedly, because of course, we didn't have anybody that we could switch out on him. You didn't want Phil Hubbard [guarding Maxwell]—they had him in foul trouble, he had four fouls."

Staton's reaction to his fifth foul was undiplomatic, uttered on national TV for everyone, including his parents, to see. "Unbeknownst to me, the camera was right in my face," Staton says, "and I gave a profane diatribe unto the nation. No sound, of course, but you didn't [need it]. So my mother was like, 'You were really mad, weren't you?' I said, 'Yeah, I'm sorry, mom, I'm sorry.' They had never heard me curse before."

With Maxwell scoring 11 of UNC's final 20 points, the 49ers built a 10-point lead with 2:10 left before Michigan rallied within four points.

Steve Grote rebounds for the Wolverines. *BL017179, Bentley Historical Library, University of Michigan.*

Green then missed the front end of a 1-and-1 with 50 seconds remaining to seal Michigan's doom in a 75–68 loss.

"It was very disappointing, very disappointing to end it all that way," Grote says. "I could much easier have accepted losing in the Final Four. Very disappointing to not get there."

The loss gave Michigan a 26-4 overall record and marked the end of a four-year run that came close to matching the Buntin-Russell era, as U-M won two conference titles and made a then-school record four straight NCAA tournament appearances, thanks to a combination of big talent and the relentless pressure of Michigan's little guys, led by Britt and Grote.

"It's just my observation," Grote says, "that the strongest personalities on a basketball team, that style of play oftentimes becomes the norm. And with me and Wayman Britt playing basically the same style, I think it became a scenario where, if you didn't play like that, you didn't get in the lineup; it just kind of took on a life of its own…where it became contagious. We just became a very high-pressure, aggressive, defensive team. And it's fun to play that way. There's nothing better than taking the other team out of their game because you're so good on defense."

Grote and Britt's legacies were preserved as Michigan named its top defender award after Britt and its hustle award after Grote. "You appreciate it the older you get," Grote says. "You know that it's a chance then for your name to live on forever and ever and ever. And you know, I was a good player; I was not a great player. I played on great teams, and I think that I helped make our teams great. But my number was never going to be hanging from the [rafters]. But I do think that I did something that no one else had done before in the program's history, which was to just absolutely leave it all on the floor almost every game."

Declining Years

The downward trajectory of Johnny Orr's last three years at Michigan began in the 1977 offseason. First, the nation's prize high school recruit, Magic Johnson, selected Michigan State over U-M. Although Johnson lived in Lansing, in MSU's backyard, he had still received Frieder's high-octane recruiting offensive.

"There's nobody that recruited Magic harder than I did," Frieder says. "And Magic will tell you that.…Long story short, his parents wanted him to go to Michigan State, and the job that Michigan State did and the pressure that the town put on him, and his parents, that's where he ended."

Staton—who was acquainted with Johnson before he signed with MSU—says that had Magic hailed from some other Michigan city, he might've become a Wolverine. "He wanted to be a Michigan Man," Staton says, "but coming out of Lansing, I think the circumstances were such that it was better for him to go to Michigan State."

Then, during the summer, Hubbard injured his knee playing for the U.S. team in the World University Games. Later, his knee gave out on the first day of Michigan's preseason practice. He underwent surgery and was out for the season.

With Hubbard out, freshman Mike McGee tried to fill the void as U-M's key scorer. Orr had been impressed with the 6-foot-5 McGee from the moment he watched the Omaha native play. "I went out there to see him play, he made 57 points," Orr recalls. "And we were very fortunate to get Mike. He was an offensive machine. We had to find someplace for him on defense, but on offense, he could play."

The combination of Hubbard's injury and McGee's arrival transformed the team for the remainder of Orr's tenure. For the previous two years, "our strength was team chemistry, the ability to come together," Staton explains. But with Hubbard gone, the team quickly began revolving around the sharp-shooting but inexperienced McGee.

Mike McGee was Michigan's scoring star for four years. *BL016959, Bentley Historical Library, University of Michigan.*

"He had a lot of learning to do as far as our offense and defense, etc.," Staton says. "And it took almost a half a season for things to gel. We had team meetings and everything. But Johnny Orr and those guys said, hey, we told him when he came here that he would start every game in a Michigan uniform. So, there are green lights and there are green lights—and [McGee] set the record for field goal attempts for a freshman in the Big Ten. Need I say more? Love him to death, but it was something different."

McGee scored 19.7 points per game that season, which still stands, as of 2023, as Michigan's freshman scoring record. In addition to his deadly jumper, McGee had something of the Tomjanovich-Wilmore-Robinson instinct on the offensive glass.

"He was one of the toughest 6-5 post men that the Big Ten has ever seen," Staton says. "He was like Adrian Dantley. I remember when [McGee] was playing for the [NBA Los Angeles] Lakers, the announcer said, 'That Mike McGee, he'll crawl over his grandmother's back to get an offensive rebound.' He just had a love of scoring. He lived to score. And was very good at it as well. But it did take us some time to adjust to that, and our record suffered because of that, especially in the Big Ten."

Michigan remained a solid, winning team in Orr's last three seasons but received no further NCAA bids. Meanwhile, Magic Johnson's Spartans won two Big Ten titles plus the 1979 NCAA championship. But Michigan battled MSU to a head-to-head draw in Magic's two college seasons, winning a pair of last-second nail-biters. In 1978, Mark Lozier sank a 29-footer at the buzzer to give the visiting Wolverines a 65–63 victory. At Crisler the following season, Johnson fouled U-M freshman Keith Smith as time ran out. Smith sank the front end of the 1-and-1 opportunity to seal a 49–48 Michigan win.

Hubbard Comes and Goes

Hubbard returned for the 1978–79 season, playing with a knee brace, but he wasn't quite as quick as he'd been previously. Additionally, the team's chemistry wasn't as strong as before. Why? "Because Mike took all the shots and didn't pass it to anybody. That might be why," Hubbard says. "That might've been it right there, because you had Tommy and Alan [Hardy] who were pretty good players. But it just happened to be that way.…[McGee] was a scorer. He scored in high school, he scored in college. That's all he knew."

Hubbard left for the NBA after the season and was drafted by Vitale, who was then coaching the Detroit Pistons. "They never really saw the real Phil Hubbard in the NBA," Staton says. "He literally drug his knee around with a brace for 10 years and still was a damn good player."

In January 2004, Hubbard became the third Wolverine to receive the school's highest basketball honor, as his no. 35 jersey was lifted to Crisler Arena's rafters to join Cazzie and Rudy T among Michigan's elite stars.

In Orr's final year, 1979–80, McGee led Michigan in scoring while Thad Garner did just about everything else. Blossoming in his sophomore year, the 6-foot-7 forward led Michigan in an unlikely trifecta: rebounds, assists and steals.

Garner "was a great runner," Orr says, "6-7 and he could run the floor and play defense, good offense. A good player. Very good. Not big and strong; he was a skinny kid. But he was an awful good basketball player."

Michigan's highlight victory of 1979–80 was an overtime triumph over second-ranked Ohio State on a Lozier free throw. U-M finished 17-13 overall, 8-10 in conference play, and earned its first NIT berth since 1971. In the previous two years, postseason opportunities had almost doubled: the NCAA field expanded from 32 to 40 and then to 48 teams, while the NIT went from 16 schools to 24 and then 32.

The NIT schedulers handed Michigan a pair of home games. Against Nebraska, Michigan expanded a 3-point halftime lead to 50–37 on its way to a 76–69 victory. Michigan then had little trouble with UTEP in a 74–65 victory before traveling to the University of Virginia for a 79–68 loss.

THERE GOES JOHNNY

The 1979–80 season was Orr's twelfth as Michigan's head coach. He seemed set in his position and said as much to key recruit Tim McCormick shortly after the season ended. "The week before I had asked Johnny Orr about the rumors that he was going to Iowa State, and he said, 'They're absolutely false, I will be your coach for four years if you commit to Michigan,'" McCormick says.

There's no reason to believe that Orr's reassurance was anything but sincere. Circumstances, however, changed during the following week. Iowa State coach Lynn Nance had resigned earlier, and the school was searching for a replacement. Army head coach Mike Krzyzewski interviewed for the post, but he took the Duke job instead—and who knows how U-M basketball history might've changed if Coach K had taken the Iowa State job and not gone to Duke, and Orr had remained at Michigan.

Orr's part in the Iowa State saga began when Iowa State officials contacted him only—they said—to ask for his advice. Frieder notes that "the first call that Johnny Orr made to Iowa State was for me, to tell 'em they ought to interview Bill Frieder." But Iowa State officials told Orr they wanted someone with head coaching experience and then asked if he'd tour the school's facilities so he could recommend the job to another candidate. But after the tour, he was offered the head coaching job.

"And I said, 'No, no, I've got a good job. And I'm not going to be coaching that much longer,'" Orr recalls. "So I went back to Ann Arbor, and I went in and told Canham I needed a raise. And he didn't give me a raise. So I was disappointed in that. And I talked to my wife [Romie], and she said, 'Did you like [Iowa State]?' I said, 'The people were wonderful around me. They were really nice.'"

Shortly after telling McCormick he'd be returning to Michigan, Orr received another invitation from Iowa State. This time, he toured the campus with Romie and then met with school president Dr. W. Robert Parks, who told Orr that he was a "basketball nut" who wanted "a good team before I retired." Finally, Orr recalls, Park told Iowa State athletic director Lou McCullough, "'Anything Johnny wants, you give it to him.' And I shook his hand, I said, 'Dr. Parks, I'm your coach.'"

Orr earned $33,500 at Michigan—reportedly in the lower tier of Big Ten basketball head coaching salaries—while Iowa State's six-year contract paid him $52,000 annually. He also received money for radio and TV shows, plus free use of Iowa State's facilities for his basketball camp.

Although he worked on a handshake deal at Michigan, Orr says he "never doubted" that Canham would retain him. "As long as I wanted to be there, I would've been there with Canham." He adds that Canham "couldn't have been a better guy to work for. That's the only thing he ever turned me down on, was when I wanted a raise and he wouldn't give it to me."

At the time of his retirement in 1994, Orr was the winningest coach in both Michigan and Iowa State basketball history, with a 209-113 record at Michigan and a 218-200 mark at Iowa State. As of 2023, he's second to John Beilein on the U-M list but remains on top of the Cyclones'. He was honored by both schools during the 2010–11 season. Iowa State dedicated a statue of Orr in its arena, while U-M inducted Orr into Michigan's athletics Hall of Honor. Orr passed away in 2013 at age eighty-six. The man who brought him to Michigan, Dave Strack, died a year later at age ninety.

FRIEDER AND THE FIRST FABS, 1980–1984

As Michigan's lead assistant in the late '70s, Bill Frieder received some Division I head coaching offers but turned them all down, partly due to Don Canham's prodding. "Don Canham just would say, 'Hey, I don't want to hear about this,'" Frieder says. "'You're nuts. You're going to be the next Michigan coach.' So he'd laugh about me on some of these jobs." True to his word, Canham named Frieder to replace the departed Orr.

Frieder, thirty-eight, was already famous for not wasting time on non-basketball activities. Off the court, he ate fast, drove fast and slept little. "He was a workaholic," recalls George Pomey, who drove with Frieder on some recruiting trips. "He took recruiting to a new level."

On the court, "He was a player's coach," recalls Butch Wade, echoing other Frieder-coached players. "He didn't try to pull the reins back or hold the ball or run any Princeton offense. He just let us play."

Tim McCormick was Frieder's top recruiting target in 1980. A skilled 6-foot-11 center, McCormick gave U-M its first premier big man since Phil Hubbard. The Clarkston, Michigan native also represented the direction Frieder wanted to take U-M recruiting.

"The day I took the job," Frieder recalls, "we did not have one Michigan kid on our roster….That was all of our fault. I think we had the success that we had, and we started recruiting nationally. And we'd miss out on national kids like Clark Kellogg [who attended Ohio State] and others, and because we didn't do what we were supposed to do in Michigan, we were losing the good Michigan players. So I decided, the day I became head coach, I'm going to go after the top two kids in Michigan every year."

McCormick was a coveted recruit who had his choice of major schools, but Frieder used the home-state angle to help secure his services. "My final decision was Michigan/North Carolina," McCormick says, "and I remember on Christmas morning my senior year I received a call....Coach Frieder said, 'How are you enjoying Christmas morning with your family?' And I said, 'It's great. We just opened presents, and we're going to have a Christmas breakfast together.' And he said, 'OK, great. I just wanted to let you know that next year North Carolina is in a Christmas tournament at home, and so one year from now, if you go to North Carolina, you're going to be 649 miles away from home and the cost of a plane ticket is currently $472, and you're going to be sitting in a dorm room by yourself.' And he said, 'Why don't you go back to enjoying your family and have a merry Christmas.'"

Frieder's message resonated with McCormick, who signed with Michigan the following spring. "Tim was a delight because he was just such a quality kid," Frieder says. "And he was a big 7-foot kid that could shoot the basketball. He had a great touch. He knew how to play."

"He was like a guard on the court when it came down to basketball," says three-year teammate Leslie Rockymore, "just telling you where you need to be."

But like many freshmen, McCormick struggled in his first season. "When I came to college, I just kind of assumed that I was going to be the best player on the court against anybody I faced," McCormick explains. "I had never played against anybody as big as me. And my freshman year I was just overwhelmed."

Additionally, McGee remained Michigan's star, and he wasn't shy about letting the rookie know it. McCormick calls McGee "the best-conditioned athlete that I ever played with. I never saw anybody that could run as fast and as long as Mike McGee. And I also felt, he was probably 30 to 40 percent faster going to the offensive end than to the defensive end. I also remember before my first game, I was so excited to finally be a Michigan Wolverine. I ran out of the tunnel, and they were playing the fight song and I found my family. It was a dream come true. And Mike came up to me right before the game, and he said, 'Listen, you're only a freshman and I'm a senior. I'm going to be the Big Ten's all-time leading scorer this year. If you get the ball, don't shoot. Throw it to me. You can score the next year.'

"He was dead serious. I kind of laughed and said, 'Really?' And he said, 'Yes.' He wasn't joking."

Tim McCormick became Bill Frieder's first big recruit as head coach. *BL013102, Bentley Historical Library, University of Michigan.*

Michigan was 9-0 in the 1980–81 pre-conference season and then won four overtime games on the way to a 7-3 Big Ten start. But the team wore down at the end of the season and finished just 8-10 in conference play. "I think what got us is just the rigors of the Big Ten," Frieder recalls. "Being a first-year head coach, I probably made mistakes that I didn't make after that, with game preparation and reacting the right way after wins and losses, etc. So, I probably learned a lot those first couple years."

A 17-10 overall mark earned U-M an NIT berth, beginning with two home games. McGee scored 26 points in a 74–58 Michigan victory against Duquesne, and then U-M pulled away in the second half to beat Toledo three days later, 80–68, behind McGee's 25 points and Johnny Johnson's 22, before dropping a 91–76 decision at Syracuse.

McGee went out gunning, hitting 14 of 27 shots for 30 points in his last game. He achieved his goal and left Michigan as the Big Ten's all-time scoring leader with 2,439 career points. McGee retained the record until the final game of Glen Rice's career. As of 2023, he's second in points and fifth in career scoring average (21.3) on Michigan's all-time list.

Rebuilding

McGee and Michigan's remaining starters, except for Thad Garner, graduated in 1981, so the next two seasons were devoted to recruiting and rebuilding the team.

Additionally, McCormick's development was delayed, as he missed the 1981–82 season after undergoing surgery on both his knees, leaving the 6-foot-7 Garner to play center.

The bright spot in Frieder's second year was the development of homegrown freshman guards Eric Turner, from Flint, and Detroit's Rockymore.

Garner, meanwhile, was Michigan's ultimate unheralded player. Despite his versatility and production, he never received any All–Big Ten notice. But he was appreciated by teammates and coaches, and after his graduation, U-M named its leadership award in his honor. "Thad Garner was the leader," Rockymore says. "Thad kind of took me, Eric, up under his wing. He spent a lot of time with us, taught us a lot about the things that happen in the Big Ten."

As Michigan moved through a 7-20 season in 1981–82 (later changed officially to 8-19 due to a Wisconsin forfeit), Frieder and his staff sought a brighter future on the recruiting trail. Following his team-building blueprint,

Frieder signed his first Michigan Mr. Basketball award-winner, Robert Henderson. Frieder lured the Lansing Eastern star away from MSU because Michigan had his desired academic program. Frieder used Michigan football connections to recruit Butch Wade, from Massachusetts, and Richard Rellford, who attended the same Florida high school as Michigan football great Anthony Carter.

But Frieder paid the football team back by bringing in a fourth recruit, Paul Jokisch, another in-state product from Birmingham Brother Rice High School. Jokisch signed a basketball scholarship with the understanding that he could also play football, but he eventually left the basketball team after two seasons and became a productive U-M wide receiver.

Unlike the first four, the fifth player in the 1982 class wasn't a highly rated recruit. Indeed, he was almost unknown, even after a solid senior high school season at Detroit Cooley. But he became the standout of the class, as well as of the Big Ten.

"I came here as a ghost," Roy Tarpley later told *Sports Illustrated*. He was so eager to accept Frieder's scholarship offer that he didn't bother to visit Ann Arbor—or anywhere else. Before his senior year of high school, Tarpley had moved from Alabama to Detroit, where Frieder spotted him playing in the St. Cecilia's summer league.

"He was only like 6-6, 6-7 then," Frieder says, "but I kept telling my staff, 'This kid's going to grow, he's going to get better.' So we recruited him. He surprised us, he said, 'I want to come to Michigan.' So he ended up being the best player out of that class. And we didn't have to beat anybody on him. We just got him."

The local media then decided that a five-player class of big men—Rellford was the shortest at 6-foot-6—deserved its own nickname. "We were the original 'Fab Five,'" Butch Wade recalls. But what the media gave, it could take away. Without the quick success of the later quintet with the same name, the nickname faded away quickly.

Once the five were on campus, the veterans—young though they were—took the rookies in hand and helped mentor them through their freshman campaign. Rockymore explains that he, McCormick and Turner "really made up our minds—'Look, we want to win.' And the way we win is that we have to teach the younger guys. And some of them, put up under our wing and be with them on a daily basis to help them get that Big Ten transition."

Rellford and Henderson had the biggest immediate impacts, as Rellford started 22 of the 28 games and was fourth on the team in scoring, while Henderson started 17 times and was second in rebounding.

Butch Wade gets ready to slam it home for Michigan. *BL015738, Bentley Historical Library, University of Michigan.*

Gary Grant, who joined the team in 1984, says Rellford "was just a down, gritty player that played so hard, and he always wanted to either shoot the jump shot, from the corner, or dunk on you underneath, on two-feet dunkers."

Henderson, meanwhile, "was not a 'Basketball Jones' personality," recalls Loy Vaught, who was a freshman in Henderson's senior year. "He was a guy with a lot of interests. He had sort of a different mentality about it. A lot of the other guys, their identities were all, 'I'm a Michigan basketball player.' And his identity was, 'I'm a Michigan basketball player, but that's just one of the things that I do. I'm multi-talented kind of a guy.'"

The 6-foot-8 Wade got off to a slow start that season but was a solid contributor in the Big Ten campaign, and he added a physical presence to Michigan's front line.

"Butch was the enforcer," says Antoine Joubert, who joined the team the following season. "Butch would do all the things that people don't recognize, all the rebounding, setting screens when guys are denying you the ball and making you work hard. Butch is like, 'Run it by me, I'll get you open.' Getting the rebounds, stepping in, taking charges. None of those things show up on the stat sheet besides the rebounds, but you've got to have a guy like that."

A less-publicized addition to Michigan's family that year was an assistant coach whom Frieder hired away from Western Michigan: Steve Fisher. Frieder and Fisher had met at the 1975 NCAA tournament, and Fisher was later interviewed by Orr for an assistant's job at U-M. "Some time before I became head coach, I knew he was a guy that I would consider hiring if I ever became a head coach," Frieder says.

Growing Up

Michigan finished 15-13 in the 1982–83 season, which featured an unusual visitor. After losing 93–76 at Indiana, Frieder asked Bob Knight to speak to his team. Knight grabbed the players' attention when he told the Wolverines to hold their heads high, that better times were ahead. "He did a fantastic job for me," Frieder says.

Rockymore says that Knight "came in and told us that he thought our team had something special because of the talent level….And I think from that point it kind of let us know that we can go out and beat any team that we face."

The summer of 1983 was a busy one for McCormick, as he began working out with the Michigan football team to strengthen his surgically repaired knees. Additionally, he was confronted by Frieder, who, McCormick says, told the big man that he'd been "a major disappointment," after averaging 12.3 points and 6.4 rebounds per game the previous season. Frieder then told McCormick, "'If you don't become our starting center and have the kind of year that you're capable of, I'm not going to have you back for your last year at Michigan. I'm not going to give you your redshirt year.' And that was pretty devastating to me, but it was really a great wake-up call. I came from a really nice background. There was not a lot of tension or trauma—there were no problems. So this is one of the first times I had somebody really challenge me. And it made me mad, and it gave me a single-minded focus that I was going to have a great year and a great career. And I intensified my workouts, and my goal was that one day I would be able to tell Bill Frieder that I'm not coming back for my last year."

With the big five recruits from 1982 all back the following season, along with an energized McCormick, Michigan was loaded with talent up front. Additionally, Frieder signed the state's top high school player in 1983, guard Antoine Joubert. But the big story of 1983–84 was the development of Roy Tarpley.

Tarpley was no longer the 6-foot-6 skinny kid Frieder first spotted two years earlier. He was now 6-foot-11 and closing in on his eventual NBA playing weight of 230 pounds, after adding about 20 pounds of muscle in the previous year.

Tarpley improved because "he got bigger, he got stronger, he learned how to play," Frieder says. By the end of his sophomore season, "he became a dominant post player. And he was long and lengthy and quick, man, and explosive."

Tarpley was also a high-IQ basketball student. "He was a joy to work with because all you had to do was show him something, the next thing you know he's doing it in the game," says Mike Boyd, a U-M assistant from 1978 to 1990. "There's a lot of kids, you show them something, they have to work on it. Then once you work on it, then you've got to get to the stage that you feel so confident with it that you actually use it in a game. With Roy, you show him something in practice, he may do it a few times in practice, then all of the sudden, in a game, in the heat of the battle, he'd do it."

Tarpley's story emerged over the course of the season. As the year began, however, the headlines went to Joubert.

The Judge Takes the Court

Joubert, Rockymore's friend and former prep teammate, spent much of his high school career in the national spotlight. Some observers ranked him as the top high school player in the country and the best player from the state since Magic Johnson.

"I did have a little concern about his quickness," Frieder says. "But boy he could score, and he was a big-time player. And at that time for us, he was a big-time name. And I thought for the credibility of my program, we had to have Joubert. So he was a huge signing."

Joubert's friendship with Rockymore gave Michigan an edge in the recruiting battle, but Frieder, of course, took no chances. While attending a Detroit Southwestern High practice, Frieder overheard head coach Perry Watson—a future U-M assistant—talk with Joubert about attending that night's Detroit Pistons game. Later at the game, Watson recalls, "I just kind of looked across the arena, and I see a guy going up and down aisles. And as he got a little closer I said, 'Antoine, that's Bill Frieder.' He was walking up and down every aisle until he found Antoine. And [Joubert] was on the end seat and I was on the inside seat, and [Frieder] sat on that concrete step the whole game, sitting next to Antoine, talking. And I thought, 'Man, this guy's not going to miss a beat.'"

Joubert brought national notoriety and his unique nickname—"The Judge"—to Michigan. But the nickname had nothing to do with the basketball court. He gained the tag as a child because of his resemblance to a great-uncle who was also called "The Judge."

As for the fame, it was clear from the start that neither his press clippings nor his high-scoring prep style would affect Joubert's play for the Wolverines. "He was very unselfish," McCormick says. "He was such a gunner in high school that people, they kind of think of him as a one-dimensional player. But he actually left Michigan as the all-time assist leader. And he gave us a real swagger....He had a good type of cockiness, like, 'Give me the ball, I'll make big plays for you.'"

In 1983–84, U-M transitioned from a guard-oriented team to an offense that went inside first. Tarpley and McCormick were the top scorers, but Wade also had a key role. Prior to the season, Wade says, the coaches explained that Wade's job would be "banging and rebounding and playing tough inside." Wade says he was "fine and comfortable doing that," adding, "My motto was always, 'Be the guy that was inflicting the pain, not the guy taking the pain.'"

The transition to a post-oriented offense meant fewer shots for Turner, who'd led Michigan in scoring his two previous years. But like Joubert, Turner was willing to share the ball. "It really didn't matter to him," Rockymore says. "I think Eric wasn't even worried about being the leading scorer."

Defensively, Frieder maintained a man-to-man preference despite Michigan's size. "We played man, and we were good at it," Joubert says. "You had to really be clicking to get us on a given day....We had good defenders, I mean all around. We were big and strong and fast."

Michigan started 8-0 before losing a pair of 1-point games and then enjoyed Frieder's first winning Big Ten season. With Tarpley and McCormick playing together—McCormick had accepted Frieder's challenge and earned the starting nod—Michigan had two big men who could either post up or drift outside for a mid-range shot. Both were also sharp passers. "It was a double post," McCormick explains. "We shared the job. He was pretty versatile, and I could move around and handle the ball and pass. So we complemented each other very well."

"Our goal was to get the ball inside to them and let's see what happens," Joubert says. "There was no shot clock, no 3-point shot, so making long shots really didn't count that year."

On the other end, Tarpley proved a dangerous defender. He blocked 69 shots that season—he eventually set Michigan's school record of 97 as a senior—and changed uncounted others. His presence in the paint also let U-M's perimeter players stay tighter on defense—if they were beaten off the dribble, the ballhandler was still faced with the Tarpley-McCormick gauntlet.

STEPPING STONE

Michigan began its return to Big Ten prominence with a solid 1984 conference season, starting with a 55–50 home-court victory over Indiana. The Wolverines later beat Ohio State on the road to begin a four-game winning streak. Tarpley led the way with 24 points and 12 rebounds and held Buckeyes forward Tony Campbell to 5-for-14 shooting. McCormick recalls the game as a key moment in Tarpley's development.

"As a freshman, Roy was really skinny, and he was weak," McCormick says. "He covered me in practice, and I was able to push him around and be very physical with him. And then, as he got older, all of a sudden he added strength. He started to have some good practices, and he fought back. At Ohio State, I had early foul trouble in the first half, and they put Roy in the

Les Rockymore handles the ball during the Wolverines' 1984 NIT championship run. *BL015257, Bentley Historical Library, University of Michigan.*

game for me and…the light clicked. He figured out how good he was. We could see him coming on in practice. And basically from that point on, he became the best big man in the Big Ten."

Michigan closed the conference season at Northwestern, likely needing a victory to secure an NCAA tournament bid. With the score 52-all in overtime, Michigan played for the last shot, but Rockymore's mid-range attempt was off the mark. John Peterson rebounded, and Tarpley fouled him with four ticks left on the clock. Peterson sank both free throws, and then Turner's 23-footer rimmed off the hoop at the buzzer, ending the Wolverines' NCAA hopes. Nevertheless, Michigan's 10-8 Big Ten record—later upgraded to 11-7 officially due to a Wisconsin forfeit—was the Wolverines' best conference mark since 1978, and their 18-10 regular season record earned U-M a spot in the NIT.

A disappointed NCAA bubble team typically goes into the NIT either gunning for a championship or just playing out the string. McCormick didn't want to play out the string. "Our first practice, I talked to our team about the opportunity to win a championship," McCormick says. "A lot of teams don't want to play in the NIT. I said, 'I want to win this thing.'"

Unlike previous NIT experiences, Michigan played three home games, which proved decisive. With the NIT's 45-second shot clock in place, Michigan's first opponent, Wichita State, tried to press Michigan, but the Wolverines shredded the press, and kept shredding it, cruising to a 94–70 victory. Game two opponent Marquette stayed close most of the way, rallying from eight down to within 64–62 with 4:08 left, but U-M hit 15 of its final 17 free throws to secure an 83–70 victory.

Next was Xavier, which had knocked Ohio State out of the tournament. In front of a noisy Crisler crowd of 12,178, the small but quick Musketeers pressed—much more effectively than Wichita—and also zoned to try to limit Michigan's inside game. But thanks to late free throws by Tarpley and Joubert, Michigan moved on to New York with a 63–62 victory.

Michigan met an up-tempo Virginia Tech squad in the NIT semifinal and trailed by nine in the opening half. But when center Bobby Beecher left with four personals in the second half, Tech went to a zone. Led by Joubert, Michigan shot them out of it, as the Wolverines grabbed a 60–58 edge. The game see-sawed through the final minutes until Tarpley hit both ends of a 1-and-1 with 45 seconds left for a 76–75 lead. Tech missed a shot, and then Tarpley boarded and fed Joubert for the insurance bucket that sent Michigan to victory, 78–75.

At 21-11, Notre Dame was favored in the final, but the Irish had no answer for the inspired McCormick. The first half was tight, as U-M couldn't get its inside game into full throttle. McCormick shot well early, but Tarpley was just 1-for-7 in the half, which ended with the Wolverines holding a 28–26 edge. Michigan then hit its first nine shots of the second half, on its way to a 19-for-26 second-half shooting performance. A 20–2 run sealed the deal as McCormick posted 28 points and 14 rebounds, earning the NIT's MVP trophy in an 83–63 victory.

"I had a lot of fun," McCormick says. "I got off to a quick start, gained confidence. It was the feel-good game of my career." McCormick was academically a senior in 1983–84 but had a year of eligibility remaining because he'd missed a season following his surgeries. Despite his vow to spurn Frieder and leave after four years, McCormick applied to U-M's graduate school and planned to return the following season. But the day before the NIT final, McCormick found out that he wasn't going to be accepted into U-M's grad school.

"I was very disappointed in that," McCormick says. "I didn't want to just come back and not take classes. I already had my degree. So when I walked into the locker room, I knew at that moment that I was gone" to the NBA, where he enjoyed an eight-year career. But his NIT performance had given the program momentum that helped lead to greater success in the following seasons.

BUILDING TOWARD THE SUMMIT, 1984–1988

Frieder hoped that Michigan's NIT championship would be a stepping stone toward greater success. His hopes appeared to take a hit when not only McCormick but also lead guard Eric Turner left early for pro basketball. But looks could be deceiving, as Frieder had Turner's replacement standing by: Gary Grant.

"I loved his work ethic as a high school player," Frieder says. "I really thought, if we got Gary Grant, it didn't matter who we lost" at the guard spot.

Frieder deviated a bit from his Michigan-first recruiting philosophy for the 1984 class by focusing on Grant, a Canton, Ohio product from McKinley High, the same school that produced Phil Hubbard. But while Frieder believed that Grant would start, the freshman was less certain. "I didn't think so, but I had enough confidence in my own game that I knew if I didn't start, I would play a lot of minutes," Grant says. Unlike most young players, Grant's confidence flowed from his defensive ability, a skill he learned by necessity.

"When I was growing up, playing against my [older] brothers...the only way I could beat 'em was if I could try to stop 'em," Grant says. "My mentality the whole time was, anybody I played with, I tried to stop them, to give me more opportunities to score, until my offensive game caught up."

At Michigan, Grant usually defended the opponent's highest-scoring guard, beginning in his freshman season. "He was an unbelievable defensive player," Boyd says, adding that in high school "he was more of a 2-guard than a point guard. We moved him over to the point, and all of a sudden,

Gary Grant (no. 25) and Loy Vaught (no. 35) defend against Purdue. *BL019452, Bentley Historical Library, University of Michigan.*

with the skills he had being a defender and the [offensive skills], he ended up being an unbelievable point guard that could put the ball in the basket."

One key to Grant's seamless transition to college was his backcourt partnership with Joubert. Grant, though a well-known recruit, didn't receive Joubert-level hype. With Joubert stepping up in his first season as a full-time starter, Grant moved somewhat under the radar, at least until his talent became evident.

"I wouldn't have wanted anybody else to play those first two years with me, more so than Antoine Joubert," Grant explains, "because he took a lot of pressure off of me. Because they were trying to double-team him, and they knew who he was, and I was just a guy from Canton, Ohio, trying to fit in."

And, like Joubert, Grant came with a distinctive nickname, as hometown media had dubbed him "The General"—inspired by Civil War general and fellow Ohioan Ulysses S. Grant.

Michigan began the season 8-1, as the Judge and the General blended well in the backcourt. But their friendship also had its competitive side, as Loy Vaught witnessed during Joubert's senior season. Joubert "liked to talk a lot when he played," Vaught says. "He loved to be challenged, he loved to issue a challenge, and he's a Detroit guy….He'd be challenging Gary to one-on-one and telling Gary [that] Gary can't stop him. Gary took a lot of pride in defense. So he'd be telling Gary that he better be glad they're on the same team because he'd bust him up if they were on opposing teams."

While Grant was technically the point guard that season, Joubert handled the ball a bit more often and led the team in assists, averaging 5.7 per game to Grant's 4.7. With two skilled ballhandlers in the backcourt, four Wolverines posted double-digit scoring averages in each of the next two years, as Joubert and Grant spread the ball around. Michigan combined talent with unselfishness and featured its most physical group since the days of Bloody Nose Lane. "I used to call [Rellford and Wade], when they played together, the Bruise Brothers," Boyd says, "because they were physical. We had, probably, the two most physical bookends in the league that year."

The final piece of the puzzle was Michigan's experience. The Wolverines lost several tight games the previous season, including a four-overtime heartbreaker at Illinois. But Joubert believes that Michigan grew up during the previous year's nail-biters. "You have to learn how to be in situations where the game is tight," Joubert says. By the 1985 Big Ten season, Michigan had learned its lesson, as the Wolverines won seven conference games by seven points or fewer.

Masters of the Big Ten

The days of the minutes-long stall were nearly over in 1985 as the Big Ten instituted a 45-second clock. The NCAA did the same the next season. But the time limitation wasn't a factor when preseason co-favorite Indiana blew Michigan out in the conference opener, 87–62. The 12th-ranked Hoosiers won in large part by focusing on Tarpley, holding him to 12 points on 4-for-15 shooting. With McCormick gone to the NBA, Tarpley was now, in Frieder's words, "a marked man" as Michigan's lone post player.

Michigan bounced back with an 87–82 victory over visiting Ohio State and then lost its first conference road game at no. 15 Illinois, the other Big Ten co-favorite, 64–58 in overtime.

Looking back at Michigan's 1-2 conference start, Rockymore says the Wolverines needed to change their attitudes and work habits. "I think those losses that we had kind of woke us up to saying that, 'Hey, even though we're a good team on paper, that we have to really prove it.'"

But the losses didn't erode Michigan's confidence. "We knew we had something special," Wade says. "It was just a matter of time. And when we got it going, we got it going."

Michigan then traveled to Purdue to face a strong Boilermakers team destined to tie for third in the Big Ten. Yet Michigan desperately needed to avoid starting the conference campaign 1-3.

U-M led 43–41 with 13:58 left when Frieder went to a three-guard offense, as sophomore Garde Thompson joined Joubert and Grant on the court. The trio combined for 13 points during a 15–0 Michigan run on the way to an 81–65 victory.

Offensively, Tarpley's performance was just as important as the three-guard set. He'd shot 14-for-46 in the first three Big Ten games, but he was 10-for-16 at Purdue. Beginning with the Purdue contest, Tarpley shot 53.5 percent from the field in the remaining conference schedule. "That was kind of when Roy came into his own," Wade says, "and Gary stepped up and everybody played their role perfectly. Nobody tried to do anything they couldn't do."

Frieder points to Michigan's first two conference victories as the keys to the team's success for the rest of the 1984–85 season. "Winning at Purdue was huge because who knows what would've happened if we returned home 1-3. But returning home from that Purdue game, where we never had much success, and being 2-2 we really felt good about ourselves."

"There's always a statement game in anybody's season," Grant says, "that they could look back on and say, that game right there really bonded us. And playing against a great team like Purdue made us get back on track. And from that standpoint, we didn't look back."

The Wolverines won their next seven conference games, including a triple-overtime triumph over Iowa in which a Grant steal set up Joubert's tying hoop in the first overtime, and then a Henderson block led to another Joubert tying shot in the second OT. A Tarpley put-back at the final buzzer gave Michigan a 69–67 victory. That left the Wolverines atop the Big Ten at 9-2. But Michigan had to close its schedule by playing five of seven on the road, beginning with 8-2 Iowa.

Tarpley's 7-for-7 first-half shooting plus strong second-half play from Rockymore and Thompson off the bench helped U-M edge the Hawkeyes by four points. The Wolverines then rallied from seven points down to beat Minnesota as Grant fed Wade for the winning hoop in a 66–64 contest.

Michigan, now third in the AP poll, then edged Michigan State, 75–73, to sweep the Spartans for the first time since 1977. It was also Michigan's third consecutive tight victory, by a total of eight points. In Big Ten games decided by five points or fewer, the Wolverines were 6-5 in 1984 but 7-0 in 1985.

The keys to Michigan's success in close games were "our front line now being juniors, and having two years of experience," Frieder says. "Along with the addition of Grant, who really became the glue, because he played tremendous defense, and he always seemed to do the right things offensively, whether it be push the ball and get transition baskets, or walk it up and set it up. He always made good decisions out on the court."

Michigan then clinched the Big Ten championship by beating Wisconsin, 88–68, while Iowa lost to Ohio State. "At that time, to me, the Big Ten championship was the most important thing," Frieder says. "That's kind of the way that I was brought up. That's kind of the way Michigan thought about things in both football and basketball."

"Now," Joubert says, "they have the [Big Ten] tournament. [If] you do bad during the regular season, you've still got a chance in the tournament. Back then, there wasn't a [second] chance. It was like, you've got to do it now, you've got to do it every night. And so every game counts."

Michigan closed the Big Ten season with victories at Ohio State and Indiana. It was Michigan's first-ever victory at Assembly Hall and its first win at Indiana in twenty years, and it wrapped up a 16-2 conference campaign that featured 15 consecutive Big Ten victories.

Tournament Struggles

With one exception, the NCAA tournament became an annual event for Michigan over the next dozen years. But it began as a yearly disappointment, as the Wolverines played very few strong tournament games in the mid-1980s, even when they won.

Michigan entered the 1985 tournament ranked second in the nation and was the no. 1 seed in the Southeast Regional. The Wolverines opened in Dayton, Ohio, against Farleigh Dickinson, the ECAC Metro Conference tournament champion, and nearly became the first top seed to lose to a 16th seed in NCAA tournament history.

The small and quick Knights played against their usual style by slowing the game down. Michigan, playing without a shot clock for the first time since the non-conference season, had trouble adjusting and trailed 26–20 at halftime.

Farleigh Dickinson collapsed its zone around Tarpley and built a 10-point lead with 14:24 remaining in the second half. Michigan then began hitting from outside, with Rockymore coming off the bench to nail two perimeter shots, forcing the Knights out of their zone. Michigan gained a 12-point lead, but the Knights cut the margin to two before Tarpley sealed the 59–55 victory with a pair of free throws.

Michigan's second-round opponent, 8th-seeded Villanova, entered the game with a deceptive 20-10 record that didn't fool Frieder. "I remember telling my athletic director that no one knows how good Villanova is," Frieder says. Due to Villanova's 10 losses, "it was tough to convince anybody that they were that good. And as it turned out, they proved that they were that good" by winning the NCAA championship that year. "We played 'em as well as anybody did in the NCAA tournament."

The Wildcats started three seniors and two juniors and played a patient game. They slowed the tempo and collapsed around Tarpley, who didn't receive enough help. Villanova "stalled the ball," Joubert says. "He had us on defense two, three minutes sometimes. And I just think that that took us out of our rhythm."

Michigan started slowly and trailed 30–26 at halftime. The Wolverines opened the second half with a 9–0 run, but Villanova then surged back in front after forcing several turnovers. A Joubert bucket put Michigan ahead 37–36 with 9:28 left, but the Wolverines never led again. It was 46–43 with 4:22 remaining when the Wildcats began stalling. Michigan was forced to foul, and Villanova hit its free throws—the Wildcats were 25-for-31 for the game—in a 59–55 victory.

Tarpley led U-M with 14 points and 13 rebounds, but Grant was 0-for-4 shooting with just one assist. "The first two years of my college career I didn't really play great in the [NCAA tournament]," Grant says. "Which, I was a freshman and sophomore, so it was kind of understandable. But on the other side, by playing pretty good in the regular season for those two years, I could've played a lot better at those stages."

Adding a Dash of Rice

The 1985–86 season was a milestone for Michigan, as the first players who'd cut down the nets at the Kingdome in 1989 arrived in Ann Arbor. All four newcomers would eventually be key performers, but only one made an impact in his freshman season. Loy Vaught and Mike Griffin redshirted that year, while Mark Hughes was limited to 13 games by a knee injury. The fourth new face was Glen Rice.

On the surface, Rice's commitment was another in-state recruiting coup for Frieder. In reality, Frieder was as lucky as he was good in signing Rice.

Rice was a late bloomer, and even when he began playing well in high school, he was overshadowed by some talented, older Flint Northwestern teammates. As a result, Rice was not highly recruited until his senior year, and Frieder didn't target Rice until he'd missed out on three other prospects who chose different Big Ten schools—Melvin McCants (Purdue), Lowell Hamilton (Illinois) and Roy Marble (Iowa). But then Rice caught fire as a senior, and Frieder's Plan D became a Class A recruit. "You knew in January [1985] he was going to be a great player," Frieder says.

Rice says that he "was real close to signing with Central Michigan" prior to the Wolverines' interest. "But I had always kept my mind on Michigan because I liked Michigan, I liked the guys that they were playing. I liked the fact that Michigan was always playing on TV, with the exposure there. It was a winning program."

As Rice blossomed he drew numerous suitors, including Johnny Orr, who'd signed Rice's high school teammate Jeff Grayer for Iowa State a year earlier. "We were very disappointed we did not get [Rice]," Orr says. "We were very close to getting him….I think it was a tough decision for him to make. But I think the biggest thing, it was closer to home for him."

Wade says that Rice was "soft spoken, quiet, his freshman year. Obviously, throughout his career he came out of his shell. But he just went along with the program. He probably progressed a lot faster than anybody else, in the

Richard Rellford became a leader who mentored many younger Wolverines. *BL011511, Bentley Historical Library, University of Michigan.*

sense that when he first got there, he was nothing but a catch-and-shoot type guy. As he got better, he was able to put the ball on the floor and create his own shot, and rebounded well."

Grant, in typical point guard fashion, appreciated having another strong scorer on the floor. "Just a pure shooter, just a great person," Grant says. "And he was a perfect fit to what we needed because he was a small forward that could stretch the defense. And he really helped us through a lot of the Big Ten games by hitting long shots, to just give me and Antoine different areas to penetrate and kick it out to him. Then we could use our bigs a lot more, just because of Glen, because he just stretched the defense so much."

Rice was Michigan's Mr. Basketball and led Flint Northwestern to a state championship as a senior. On a talented U-M squad, however, he had to play off the bench. But he says the transition "was easy. The thing about the seniors that we had on that team, they were leaders, and made me feel comfortable....I didn't mind learning from those guys. I didn't want to be thrown into the fire that early."

Rellford, who started at the small forward position that Rice would soon own, was a particularly valuable mentor for the freshman. "Richard Rellford, he always tried to teach me little tricks of trying to get over against certain individuals we played against," Rice says, "especially guys that were bigger than me at the time, because I was so small, a skinny kid at that time. Even when I was in my first couple years [with the NBA's Miami Heat], Richard, being that he was from the Florida area, I'd see him and he'd still give me advice then....Gary Grant, who I spent several years playing with, was another mentor. He got me pumped, made sure I always kept that intensity."

Michigan returned its starting five from the previous season, and the quintet drew all but seven starts in 1985–86. But the second unit pushed the starters hard in practice. "Practice was awesome," Rice says. "I mean, we went at it. And I think that's what made us so great of a team. We'd go in there at practice, and the starters and the second unit, no one took anything for granted, and there was no backing down in anyone. We pushed them to the brink. And there were times that we'd tell 'em, 'We're better than you guys,' knowing deep down inside they truly were better than us. But still, we had to impose that on them. And we made them fight for everything they got. And that's why they went out and were as prepared as they were for each and every game."

The Wolverines—ranked first in the preseason UPI coaches' poll—racked up some frequent flyer miles, and some impressive victories, to start the season. U-M beat Virginia Tech in Hawaii, 67–66, as Henderson drove to the hoop and scored with 20 seconds left, and then Grant blocked Dell Curry's shot with three seconds remaining. After crushing Kansas State, Michigan flew to Ann Arbor and then on to Massachusetts to beat no. 2 Georgia Tech in a turnover-filled game, 49–44.

The Wolverines weren't seriously challenged in December, winning nine straight to enter the Big Ten season 12-0.

DEFENDING THE CROWN

Joubert calls the 1986 Big Ten campaign "a tough year; good year but a tough year. Because now everybody knows you, now everybody loves to beat you, too."

Michigan was second in the polls and the consensus Big Ten favorite entering conference play. Having played nine home games plus three on neutral courts, the schedule-makers gave the Wolverines a tough place for their first true road game: Indiana's Assembly Hall.

It took a few minutes for the Wolverines to make the transition, as the 15th-ranked Hoosiers grabbed an 8–0 lead. But U-M quickly found its rhythm and reversed the margin, taking a 35–27 advantage into halftime on the way to a 74–69 victory.

After winning at Ohio State, Michigan returned home to beat no. 18 Illinois as Henderson sank a 17-footer at the buzzer off a Grant feed, and then topped no. 20 Purdue, giving the Wolverines a then-school record 16th straight victory. The streak then ended with an upset loss at Minnesota, but U-M won four of its next six to lead the Big Ten at 8-3, with Indiana (7-3) and Iowa (6-3) close behind.

Michigan suffered one more bump in the road, losing 74–59 to Michigan State at home. After three straight conference victories, Michigan and Indiana were tied for the Big Ten lead at 13-4, setting up a season-ending showdown with Bob Knight in the final conference game.

Michigan shoehorned a record 14,198 fans—including Cazzie Russell—into Crisler, with most fans undoubtedly anticipating a tight battle leading to Michigan's second straight conference crown. If so, they were half right. The Wolverines started quickly, led 44–25 at the half and never let up, routing Indiana 80–52. "We just buried 'em from the get-go.…It was just one of those things where Bill Frieder had us ready to go," Grant recalls.

Playing tough man-to-man defense, Michigan grabbed nine first-half steals, including four by Grant, and forced 20 turnovers on the day. "We knew it's always a tight fight to repeat anything," Joubert says. "It's hard to be champion. When you're on top, everybody's trying to knock you down.…We fell short the year before [in the NCAA tournament], so we wanted to come back and try to win [the Big Ten] title and the national title."

Even with the 28-point margin, the Wolverines gave some credit for the victory to the noisy, overflow Crisler crowd. "They had people sitting around the court, people sitting in the aisles," Wade says. "It was really hot. Someone said the fire marshal was coming—so what? It was amazing. It kind of came full circle in the sense that…the first game of the Big Ten season [the previous year], Indiana came into Crisler and just pounded us by quite a bit. We remembered that butt-kicking. We took that with us through our whole career, into that last game. And just kind of flipped the coin."

REUNION

Michigan entered the NCAA tournament 27-4, ranked 5th in both polls. U-M received a no. 2 seed in the West Regional and began play in Minnesota's Metrodome. If form held, the Wolverines would face 7th-seeded Iowa State and Johnny Orr in the second round.

First, Michigan had to beat Ohio Valley Conference champion Akron. The Zips had no player taller than 6-foot-6, and their starting center was a 6-foot-3 walk-on, so they seemed tailor-made for a Tarpley assault. But after Tarpley was late for a team meeting, Frieder held the big man out of the first 5:25 of the opening half and then 4:01 at the start of the second.

Frieder says he benched Tarpley because "when you're at a hotel on the road getting ready for an NCAA tournament game, when you're not on time [for a meeting], your mind's not on the right thing. And I really thought that was a big factor, having to deal with that, in us not performing as well as I would've liked. And I still thought I made the right decision. If someone is late, you can't ignore it."

Akron played a zone against the bigger Wolverines and, significantly, out-rebounded Michigan 34–28. Instead of playing keep-away, the Zips used a trapping defense to slow Michigan down and led 32–30 at halftime. Michigan edged ahead by a point midway through the second half, and then the reinstated Tarpley put back a missed free throw, was fouled and completed the 3-point play for a 52–48 lead with 8:03 remaining. Michigan maintained a 6- to 8-point lead the rest of the way in a 70–64 victory.

Rice scored 14 points in his first NCAA action, but the future NCAA tournament MVP says he "was nervous to the point where I had no idea at some times how to even play basketball, because it was such a bigger stage. I can admit that I felt out of place because of the overwhelming circumstances, the difference in the arena that I was playing in. But it was a thrill."

Iowa State, meanwhile, beat Miami (Ohio) on senior Jeff Hornacek's 26-footer at the buzzer. The Cyclones entered the second-round game 21-10 after finishing second in the Big Eight Conference. Orr had built a solid program since leaving U-M and had his team in the NCAA tournament for the second consecutive season.

Frieder hoped to employ Michigan's frontcourt power to force the speedy Cyclones into a bigger lineup. Orr wanted to feature quickness and make Michigan go smaller. In that respect, Orr got his wish, as Frieder tried to battle Iowa State's speed with a three-guard lineup at times. Unfortunately for Michigan, two of those guards couldn't find the range. While Joubert shot 5-for-8 and scored 11 points, Thompson was 0-for-4 and Grant 1-for-9.

Still, Michigan remained in the game until the final minute and was, perhaps, one defensive play away from a victory. The Cyclones led 40–31 at halftime and built the margin to 11 in the second half. Michigan never led in the half but came within 64–63 and had the ball with 1:25 left when Grant missed from 20 feet. Moments later, Hornacek threw a pass from near midcourt to Elmer Robinson, who was wide open near the hoop after a defensive miscommunication. Robinson dunked for a 66–63 lead with 1:18 remaining, and Michigan didn't get another chance to take the lead, dropping a 72–69 decision.

"That was a heartbreaker," Wade says of his last college game. "I still remember sitting in the locker room after the game, just feeling like a nightmare and not believing it's over. It took a long time for that pain to go away."

While Grant limited Hornacek to seven points defensively, Frieder still can't explain Grant's NCAA difficulties on the offensive end. "After being so dependable, game after game, and year after year, he had problems in the NCAA tournament three of his four years," Frieder says. "Very instrumental in us losing the freshman and sophomore years, that his numbers weren't what they normally were….I could never figure it out. I really observed him after the first year and all the things that he did to prepare. He worked hard. He'd get to the games or to the practices or whatever at the same time. His routines were all pretty consistent in the tournament as compared to the regular season. And it was just a mystery."

As Hughes watched from the bench, he felt that the Wolverines should've done what Frieder wanted to do from the start—take advantage of their height and put the ball in Tarpley's hands more often. But the loss helped put Michigan's eventual NCAA success in greater perspective. "That's what makes our '89 championship real special," Hughes says, "because that wasn't the most talented team I was on. I think the one my freshman year had more talent than we had [in 1989] and couldn't get it done."

THE FIRST FAB CLASS DEPARTS

The fabulous recruiting class of 1982—reduced to four after Paul Jokisch left to play football—was now exiting, after posting a four-year 91-32 record, including an NIT trophy plus two Big Ten championships. According to Rice, you can give that class partial credit for winning another title.

Roy Tarpley sets up in the low post against Northern Michigan. *BL011094, Bentley Historical Library, University of Michigan.*

"They taught us a lot, all the younger guys," Rice says. "I think at the end of the day it showed because we were in a position [to win the championship] our senior year, and we had to pull together as a team. And if it wasn't for the fact that we had been taught to keep our poise and maturity about ourselves, we probably wouldn't have been able to pull off what we did."

While some feel that Grant was the key player on Michigan's back-to-back conference championship teams, Grant points to Tarpley, calling the big man "the offensive go-to guy for us. When you needed a bucket, we had to run something through him because he had great touch....When we were in trouble, 90 percent of the time, he could come through with something good. And that's why we won those two Big Ten titles in a row, is because of the way he played."

Butch Wade says he's frequently asked to rank the post players he faced during his college and pro careers. "I say, 'I played against the best big man every damn practice, and that was Roy,'" Wade asserts. "Just a raw talent that just loved the game. A point guard in a big man's body."

Tarpley, the Big Ten player of the year in 1985, was the seventh overall choice in the NBA draft in 1986 and played in parts of six seasons for Dallas. He was highly successful on the court, but his career was hampered, and then ended, by drug and alcohol addiction. "He always told me that he was going to make it to the pros," Rockymore says. "And I told him, 'Well, one thing about it, Roy, just making it to the pros, you have to make it there, not just with your basketball skills, but you have to be strong in the mind, too, to be able to overcome any obstacles that you may encounter.'"

Frieder has denied rumors that Tarpley failed any drug tests at Michigan, while Rockymore says that Tarpley didn't show "any signs [of an addiction problem] that I noticed" at Michigan. "I was a captain of the team my senior year, and it wasn't anything that I could see."

A NEW ERA

Modern-day college basketball rules were essentially set in place in the 1986–87 season. There was a uniform 45-second shot clock, which was reduced to 35 seconds in 1993 and then 30 seconds in 2015. Also, after several years of conference experiments, the NCAA introduced a 19-foot, 9-inch 3-point arc, later extended to 20 feet, 9 inches.

The 3-point line arrived at a good time for Michigan, which had graduated its experienced post players. After playing a power game led by a strong frontcourt for three seasons, the Wolverines ran a three-guard set for most of the 1986–87 campaign, with Grant, Joubert and Thompson taking full advantage of the new rule.

"It was wonderful just to step behind the line and shoot the three," Grant says. "It was a fun addition to college basketball, and it made it where a guy had to stand out there and respect your outside shot, more so than sagging in. So it opened up the whole court. And it gave me an opportunity to get a lot more assists because the floor was more open and they couldn't crowd in and stop a lot of the penetration."

Meanwhile, Frieder continued to build toward the 1989 summit, signing two key players—although neither saw action that first season—in Terry Mills and Rumeal Robinson.

With four big men graduating, Mills, Michigan's Mr. Basketball, was the key recruit, and he received several years of all-out Frieder-stalking, beginning around the ninth grade. In high school, Mills recalls, "I'm actually going to class and in between classes, you would see Bill Frieder walking in the hallway. And all my friends were like, 'Did you see Coach Frieder walking in the hallway?' And this was one of those times where they couldn't necessarily have contact with me, but he would kind of find ways to more or less get himself involved.…You know, if you pulled into a parking structure, you wouldn't be surprised to see him with a security uniform on to hand you your ticket. He had a lot of tactical ways, and he really showed that he was very interested."

Robinson, from Massachusetts, also came highly regarded. But both freshmen were caught in the NCAA's new Proposition 48 rule. Because they'd fallen a bit short of the necessary SAT score in high school, neither Mills nor Robinson could play in their freshman year at Michigan. In the future, U-M would not admit Prop 48 players. But with Frieder's persistence, and a little help from the football coach, Mills and Robinson were both enrolled.

"It was a little stress getting those two people admitted," Frieder says. "But it's more about whether these kids can achieve academic success. Rumeal Robinson, he had a learning disability [dyslexia], but if you work hard and do all the extra work, as a learning disability student, you'll make it. And Rumeal proved me right. He did very well at Michigan, he got his degree.…Terry Mills was longer. They didn't admit Mills to school until later in August, and in all honesty—people talk about Bo and myself [having a bad relationship], but it was Bo Schembechler that called the [university] president for me and got Terry Mills admitted."

Robinson wouldn't have started that season, but he would've seen regular action for a team that eventually used a seven-man rotation. Mills, however, would have seen plenty of action at center and would've made the Wolverines a much different squad. As it was, Hughes—who played in 13 games the previous season—moved into Tarpley's old center spot. Rice, better suited for the small forward slot, had to play power forward.

Rice was a respectable rebounder as a freshman, but he took his rebounding to a new level as a sophomore. Indeed, one of Michigan's all-time great perimeter shooters took just a dozen 3-point shots in 1986–87 but led the team in rebounding with 9.2 per game.

"I knew I was always a pretty good rebounder," Rice says. "A lot of times when you think of yourself as scoring more, you don't think that you're going to be able to spend too much time down in the paint getting in position to rebound. But at the same time, it became easy because most of the time I was always moving, being able to bring bigger guys out on the perimeter a little bit more and at times post up smaller guys."

Grant says Rice was "a delight because he didn't really care about how many shots he had. He wanted the ball a lot when he was on fire, but he was unselfish. I remember seeing him, hundreds of times, where he had a wide-open jumper and he threw it down to Loy Vaught, he threw it down to Terry Mills, threw it down to Mark Hughes, for them to be happy as well."

Beginning with his freshman year, Boyd says Rice "understood what his job was. And that was surprising for a kid being so young, and coming off of being Mr. Basketball and being such a great player out of the state."

At center, Hughes and Vaught were content to do the dirty work, with little chance to put points on the board. Hughes "just did what he had to do," Grant says, "and that was just rebound the ball; he played smart, and he had great hands." Meanwhile, Vaught understood his role on a guard-oriented team. "It wasn't like we were posting the ball up to our very young, very inexperienced and raw big men at the time," he says. "We were just out there kind of running around, setting picks and screens and rebounding and shot-blocking. It was probably great for [the guards], having big men that would just run through a wall for 'em, just happy to be out there, with that college enthusiasm."

With Tarpley, Rellford, Wade and Henderson gone—and with Vaught and friends happily rebounding and setting screens—Michigan's balance of power shifted to the backcourt. As a result, the Wolverines unleashed a fully weaponized Gary Grant. After averaging 12.9 and 12.2 points per game in his first two years, The General tore through defenses to average 22.4 and 21.1 points per contest as a junior and senior, respectively.

"I had a new role that I had to take on," Grant says, "because I couldn't rely on the Roy Tarpleys and Butch Wades and all those guys, [or] Richard Rellford. So I knew I was going to have to pick up my scoring a lot more, which was fine because I had a lot of shots and stuff when I was a freshman and sophomore that I didn't take because I wanted to get it to my bigs."

The 1986–87 season "was a transition year," Frieder says, from a frontcourt-dominated team to one that would eventually become balanced, but only after the new front line gained experience.

Michigan was often explosive but also inconsistent in its 1986–87 non-conference campaign. Two early December games epitomized Michigan's play. On December 6, Michigan shot 65 percent in a 123–88 romp over Illinois-Chicago. Two days later, the Wolverines shot 38 percent in a 62–59 loss to Western Michigan.

Although U-M started 9-6 overall, 1-3 in the Big Ten, Rice says the team never despaired. "We just basically kept telling everyone, 'Look, it's going to change. We've just got to hang in there.' Obviously we're not the team we were before. We lost a lot of great players, players who played very important roles on our team.…But we figured if we kept at it, with the talent that we had, we could sneak up on some people."

Part of Michigan's success that season, Vaught believes, was the lack of respect the team received from many observers, including the pollsters who snubbed the Wolverines all year. "In situations like that…if you can kind of get that theme going, kind of get that, 'Us against the world' mentality, that can carry over and take your team a long way in the win department."

With one game left in the Big Ten season, Michigan, at 18-11 overall, 9-8 in conference, was likely on the NCAA bubble. The Wolverines rose from the bubble, however, and secured their postseason berth by not just beating but destroying no. 3 Purdue, 104–68.

A New Rival

Michigan gained the ninth seed in the East Regional and opened in Charlotte, North Carolina. On paper, the Wolverines' opponent was Colonial Athletic Association champ Navy. In reality, their only obstacle was 7-foot-1 center David Robinson, the national player of the year. Robinson scored 50 points, but his shipmates managed just 32 more as Michigan beat 8th-seeded Navy, 97–82.

Antoine Joubert lets it fly during the 1984 NIT. *BL015250, Bentley Historical Library, University of Michigan.*

"I made the decision to single-cover David Robinson and just make sure no one else from Navy hurt us," Frieder says. "And the game plan worked. He scored 50 points, but it was on 22-of-37 shooting, and those misses led to a lot of easy baskets for us."

While Robinson dominated in the paint, Garde Thompson was the master of the 3-point line. He sank nine triples—briefly an NCAA tournament record—and Grant had his best NCAA game to date with 26 points and six assists, while holding Navy point guard Doug Wojcik without a basket.

The victory earned Michigan a shot at no. 2 North Carolina, which entered the contest 30-3. The Wolverines started slowly in their first-ever meeting with the Tar Heels—who would become a regular postseason foe during the next few years—trailing 12–0 before pulling within 22–21 with 12:36 remaining in the half. But North Carolina quickly built the lead back to 34–25 and then to 60–43 at halftime.

Michigan opened the second half with a 15–4 run, including eight by Rice, to trail 64–58 with 15:58 remaining but drew no closer in a 109–97 loss. Grant, however, was strong again with 24 points, 10 rebounds and 10 assists. "It was a game there where I finally played a great offensive game in the [tournament]," Grant says. His performance marked U-M's first official triple-double. (Assists weren't recorded before the mid-'70s, so nobody knows for certain whether a strong ballhandler such as Cazzie or Campy Russell, or perhaps Wilmore, might've earned a triple-double previously.)

Joubert, meanwhile, ended his college career with 20 points. He left as Michigan's all-time assists leader with 539, although Grant would zip past him the next season. (Joubert is fourth on U-M's all-time list as of 2023.) But what Joubert cared about was winning. "I truly believe if we had the rules that they have now, we'd have won a national title," Joubert says, "maybe a couple times when I was in school, because that was our team's game, was a fast-paced, up-tempo [style]."

Joubert's career is often discussed relative to his recruiting hype. But remove the hype and you have a player who started 115 out of 127 games at Michigan, who scored fewer points than he could have because he accepted his role on four talented teams and who started for an NIT winner and two Big Ten champions.

DRESS REHEARSAL

Grant was the only Michigan senior who saw significant playing time in 1987–88. Surrounding him were all the key players who'd lead the Maize and Blue to NCAA glory the following season, including a key freshman, Sean Higgins, who took an unusual route to Michigan.

Higgins was among the nation's top-ranked high school players in 1987. He lived in Ann Arbor until age ten with his father, Earle Higgins, before going to California with his mother. He eventually signed a letter of intent to attend UCLA but then claimed that he'd done so under duress.

"And then when he got investigated by the NCAA," Frieder explains, "he told them he never wanted to go to UCLA....They verified everything he said, it was accurate, so they let him out of it. So he could go wherever he wanted. And I got a call one day from the NCAA saying that Higgins's letter to UCLA was null and void and he was free to go wherever he wanted to go, and that he wanted to go to Michigan. And I called Sean, and he just committed to us. It was like he fell out of the sky."

Grant jokes that Higgins "never saw a shot that he didn't like. Even when he wasn't playing [regularly]. I just knew that he was a great shooter, had great handles. He just didn't want to put in the extra work, but as far as him as a person and a player, I love it....Every time he played, he did what he had to do. He made some open shots, he could penetrate in and pass the ball."

Rice again led the team in rebounding in 1987–88 but now began drifting outside the arc and firing away, sinking 33 of 77 triple tries on the season. Some called Rice a natural shooter, but he also lived by the Cazzie Russell doctrine of almost nonstop hard work. "My thing was just to get in the gym and shoot," Rice says. "As far as my mechanics goes, they just came. I never really spent any time just having a coach tell me I need to do this or that better. I've always said that it was just a blessing from God, and it just matured as I matured, that's all. The more I stayed in the gym, the better off it got, the more confidence I gained."

While practicing, Rice says he "just shot from everywhere. I got off all kind of shots. Whether it was a couple steps behind the 3-point line—I made sure that every spot on that floor was not unfamiliar to me. I shot until my arm felt like it was going to just fall off at times."

Mills, meanwhile, stepped into the starting center role. "Terry Mills was a guy that you really don't see that much, at his height, that could handle the ball and could shoot with high touches and real soft touches," Grant says. "He could get the ball with his back toward the basket and do his move, turn

Terry Mills was
Michigan's multi-
talented center
for three seasons.
*BL010744, Bentley
Historical Library,
University of Michigan.*

and shoot so high that it came down all net. It could be a 10-footer to a four-footer, he had that arch on his shot. So that's what made him different from a lot of the big guys in the league."

Mills's transition to playing a low post role was challenging because he'd handled the ball more frequently in high school. Additionally, he and Robinson had to shake off the rust from their Prop 48 layoffs. But Vaught says neither Mills nor Robinson lost confidence during the previous year. "They had the attitude like they belonged there, and it's about time," Vaught says. "'Now we're going to show 'em,' and that kind of thing. We all embraced them; there was not a lot of jealousy or whatever. People kind of knew that they were waiting in the wings and that their talent was going to put them on the floor."

With Robinson starting at guard, Michigan's backcourt inexperience, beyond Grant, was a key concern. But Frieder had faith in Robinson. "Rumeal Robinson was an extremely dedicated kid," Frieder says, "and had a very strong will to do everything that you're supposed to do, mentally and physically, to get ready to play a basketball game….And everybody, when we recruited Rumeal, said…'He's not a point because he's too big; he's not quick enough. He's not a 2 because he can't shoot it. He's not a 3 because he's too small.' These are the things I kept hearing about Rumeal. But you always watched him play, and he won. He found a way to help his team win."

Hughes says Robinson "was probably the most confident player that I've played with, as far as his own ability….Now, you had some situations sometimes where he would get a little loose with the ball and over-dribble a little bit or take a few shots that were not necessarily in the offense for us. But he was also coachable. We could grab him by shirttail—'Hey, Rumeal, let's move that thing.' Then he was back on board. But he's one of the guys that I had to manage, some, as captain [in 1988–89]. Him and Sean were probably the two that I had to manage most."

Hughes became a captain the following year, but in 1987–88 Grant was Michigan's unquestioned leader, and he addressed the team before each game. While Grant was highly respected, he was also "probably as silly a person as you'll ever meet," Hughes says, admiringly. "He will get excited, he'll get fired up and get us going with those [pregame] speeches, but it's always got a little funny edge to it. He'd get up there and say something, and all of a sudden he'll mock Coach Frieder and has everybody cracking up."

At other times, however, Grant's mood was darker. "There'd be games where we knew we were supposed to be blowing teams out, and he'd come in there and he'd rip us a new butthole," Rice says. "And he didn't hold back on anything. If he had to curse you out, he'd curse you out. But we understood that, and we respected him for that."

By January 1988, Vaught was established in the starting five. But Higgins, who'd been playing regularly in a reserve role, became academically ineligible after January 1, shortening Frieder's bench. Nevertheless, U-M opened the conference season 6-1, trailing only 6-0 Purdue.

"Once we got off to that great start, started playing well, our confidence grew, our camaraderie and friendships grew," Vaught says. "Because in victorious situations, when you're winning, it's like watering a plant—all good things happen and things seem to go positive before you, all the way around."

Michigan—which was out-performing its Big Ten expectations for the second consecutive season—and no. 6 Purdue were both 7-1 in the conference when the Boilermakers beat U-M at Crisler. After four more victories, the Wolverines entered their February 27 game at Iowa one game behind 12-1 Purdue in the Big Ten. But U-M won just two of its remaining five conference games to finish 13-5. Even worse, Grant suffered a groin strain in a victory over Northwestern and wouldn't be 100 percent again for the rest of the season.

"We probably just ran out of gas," Grant says. "But we were playing so hard and so well....There's always one of those meaningful games that can push you back on track. But on the flip side, there's also meaningful games where, if you lose it can hurt your morale, and you can lose two or three more. So I think that's what happened."

Rice scored 29 in the final regular season game—a victory over Ohio State—to win the Big Ten scoring title with an average of 22.9 points per conference game, while Grant finished second at 21.3. The Crisler crowd cheered Grant's name after the OSU victory, his last home game, and insisted on a post-game curtain call. In typical Grant fashion, he jokingly told the crowd, "I love all you all. My four years here have been a great thing. If I could do it all over again...I'd go to UCLA."

ENDING THE FIRST-WEEKEND BLUES

Michigan entered the NCAA tournament ranked 10th in both polls. The Wolverines earned a third seed in the West Regional and traveled to Salt Lake City for the opening games.

Grant, determined to step up in his final NCAA appearance, was still playing with his leg wrapped. "I was probably like 80 percent," he says. "But I was not going to let that stop anything....I just had to use my body the right way, so I didn't get injured too much."

The Wolverines hoped to avoid another first-round NCAA scare as they faced Boise State. Neither Rice nor Grant scored much in the slow-paced game, but Robinson dished out seven first-half assists and Michigan pounded the ball inside to Mills, Vaught and Hughes. U-M opened a 36–20 margin at the half and maintained an 18-point cushion with about 12 minutes remaining.

From there "everything that could've gone wrong went wrong," Rice says. Boise sank 3-pointers, tightened up defensively and pulled within 61–58 with 18 seconds left. Mills missed a free throw with 13 seconds remaining, leaving the door open, but Mike Griffin rebounded a missed Boise 3-pointer, was fouled and sealed the 63–58 victory with two free throws.

Two days later, Michigan was determined to break another NCAA habit and avoid a second-round loss. "We just were focused," Rice says. "We didn't want to get bounced in the second game. We wanted to get that erased from everyone's mind. And, in order to do so, we just made it personal. We challenged ourselves. I know for sure I didn't want to go home over the summer saying, 'Man, we got bounced in the second game again.'"

The Wolverines faced 6th-seeded Florida, which entered 23-11. After shooting just seven times against Boise State, Rice lit up Florida for 39 points on 16-for-23 shooting, while Grant chucked his wrap and tallied 19 points plus 11 assists in a 108–85 victory.

"We just beat 'em from start to finish pretty good," Frieder recalls.

"We were getting back on track to maybe make something happen," Grant says. "There's always a surprising team or two in the NCAA, and we were hoping it was going to be us."

Michigan traveled to Seattle's Kingdome the following week for a reunion with no. 2 seed North Carolina. The 26-6 Tar Heels were ranked seventh in the nation and were playing in their eighth consecutive Sweet 16. Rice, meanwhile, was apprehensive entering the third-round game. "I didn't have a feeling that we as a team were going to play that well because we had spent so much energy in trying to get past that second game. And it was almost sort of like a little wind that was left out of the sails."

Michigan remained close, trailing 31–30 at halftime. Carolina edged in front early in the second half and never lost the lead, even though Michigan was in it almost until the end. U-M's last chance came with 1:12 left. With the Tar Heels leading 72–68, J.R. Reid missed the front end of a 1-and-1. Grant rebounded the miss, but Reid stole it back and then ended the possession with a put-back of a missed free throw for a 74–68 lead that turned into a 78–69 victory. "We hated for it to come to an end," Mills says. "We thought we were a better team than they were, but it just didn't work out that way, and it left a sour taste in our mouth. And it was like, 'Once we get an opportunity to do this again we're going to try to do better.'"

Michigan and Mills would get a chance to "do this again" the following year. For the moment, however, Frieder could appreciate a season in which his program had taken a step up. "I really felt good about the season," Frieder says. "We were going to have most everybody back the next year... Higgins would be back, and I really felt great about our team. When teams finally get to the Final Four, they don't jump to the Final Four from not winning a tournament game. Teams that got to the regionals the year before and have a lot of people back have a better chance of getting to the Final Four. So I thought we made the step that we needed to make, to eventually win a national championship."

But they'd have to win the championship without Grant. He left Michigan as the school's second all-time leading scorer with 2,222 points (he's fourth as of 2023). Grant dished out a school-record 234 assists as a senior, a mark that stood until 2011, and set U-M career records for assists (731) and steals (300) that still stand as of 2023. And while defense can't be measured statistically, few Wolverines—if any—ever played tougher defense than Grant.

Mills calls Grant "a guy that was an All-American, but you could really go to him and ask him anything and he would give you the right answer. Great leadership. He never carried himself like he was an All-American. He was your teammate. He was Gary Grant."

"He was the key to our winning the Big Ten championships in '85 and '86," Frieder says. "He was the glue of that team. He came in as a freshman and never took a possession off, defensively or offensively, in practice or games. He was just the ideal person to coach."

While Grant was off to the NBA—where he enjoyed a thirteen-year career—Rice was staying put. He considered leaving early for the NBA, and knew that he'd be a first-round draft choice, but chose to stay. "It crossed my mind," Rice says. "I just kind of thought, 'Let's see, if I tried to come out my junior year, where would I be?' I checked around, and people said that you could be in the top 16. So I gave it some thought and [said], 'Oh well. That sounds good.' But I just felt like I had some unfinished business."

THE MISSION, 1988–1989

Rice and fellow senior Mark Hughes were the co-captains of Michigan's landmark 1988–89 team. The pair shared a strong bond, going back to their freshman season, when they set their career goals. "Every year," Hughes says, he and Rice "would get in somebody's apartment and say, 'Hey, man, our goal—gotta win the Big Ten title, and win a national championship.' Every year we talked about it.…We did win the Big Ten our freshman year, but we hadn't since got close. We're like, 'Hey, why not?'"

Rice entered his final season "with a mindset that we can't fail. It was my senior year, and I didn't want to go out without at least having an opportunity to be in that position, to win an NCAA title."

Although he eventually spoke the words that represented the Wolverines' quest that season, Rice preferred to lead by example, and he set the tone with a vigorous conditioning program. "I kept telling myself, the whole season," Rice explains, "I need these guys to look at me and say, 'Man, this dude's not even tired.' Because if they look over there and see you as a leader tired, you slacking, then they would feel like they could do it."

Rice achieved his goal. Loy Vaught says Rice "would inspire you" with his play, adding, "You just felt like you had to keep up. He'd seem like he could run all day and never get tired."

While Rice provided inspirational leadership, and a few words now and then, Hughes was generally the voice of Michigan's leadership duo. "It was my job to get in the guys' ears and make sure that we're all on the same page," Hughes says, "make sure that we always stay focused and kept it going."

Mark Hughes attacks Wisconsin in 1989. *BL010731, Bentley Historical Library, University of Michigan.*

Meanwhile, before the season, Don Canham retired as Michigan's athletic director. Canham's retirement meant the loss of a key Frieder ally—Canham had supported Frieder during his early rebuilding years, and the coach never doubted that Canham's support would continue. He couldn't say the same about the new athletic director, Bo Schembechler.

Frieder and Schembechler had coexisted without problems as fellow coaches. Indeed, the long arm of Michigan football often served Frieder's recruiting efforts well. But many close observers felt that once Schembechler became the AD, a clash between two different types of men was inevitable—although few, if any, predicted that the collision would occur less than a year later.

Griffin Steps Up

As the season began, Rice, Terry Mills and Rumeal Robinson remained in the starting five, with Robinson filling Gary Grant's spot as the point guard. The trio was joined by Sean Higgins and, surprisingly, Mike Griffin. The third-year player from Illinois started twice and played regularly the previous season, but his presence in the starting lineup meant that both Vaught and Hughes began the early-season games on the bench.

Grant recalls Griffin as a "gritty guy. I hated playing against him in practice because he was just always in the way. Every time I tried to beat somebody to the hole, he was right there."

Griffin was a throwback to the Dan Fife/Wayman Britt/Steve Grote school of tough, team-first basketball. Except that Griffin shot the ball even less frequently than that trio. Despite playing more than 20 minutes per game, Griffin averaged just 2.7 points per contest in 1988–89, along with 2.8 assists per game.

Frieder calls Griffin "the perfect guy, in my estimation, to put with other guys that want the ball and need to score and want shots and so forth, because Mike wasn't worried about anything except what his responsibilities were. And his responsibilities were to get us into the offense, set screens, find shooters, work hard defensively, take charges [and] do all the intangibles and little things."

Both Griffin and Higgins could swing from guard to forward. But after Vaught began starting at power forward midway through the season, Griffin and Higgins basically shared the 2-guard spot, with Griffin starting and Higgins playing off the bench.

Michigan opened play in the Maui Classic with victories over Vanderbilt, Memphis and no. 4 Oklahoma. In the latter game, the Sooners pulled within 65–62 in the second half before Robinson tallied Michigan's next nine points. That scoring burst gave the Wolverines a 7-point lead that U-M never lost in a 91–80 victory. "I can remember that Oklahoma, we felt, was going to be our big test," Mills says, "and it was going to be our measuring stick….For us to beat them convincingly the way we did, we felt that this is our year."

Michigan spent most of the pre-conference season ranked second in the country and should've gone into the Big Ten season undefeated. But the Wolverines basically ignored a late-December game against Alaska-Anchorage, played in Salt Lake City, and fell to the Division II school, 70–66.

Mills recalls traveling to Utah when the team learned that preseason no. 1 Iowa had lost to Chaminade. "And we just laughed and giggled, we were like, 'Man, how did these guys lose to Chaminade?' And lo and behold here it is we go play Alaska (and lose). It was a learning tool for us and a learning tool for myself never to take a team for granted."

THE BUMPY BIG TEN RIDE

Frieder made at least one change in the starting five in each of the first four conference games as he searched for the right combination. The Wolverines won three of those games easily but lost at Illinois, 96–84.

Illinois, 15-0, was the second Big Ten team to reach no. 1 in the polls in 1988–89, although the Illini were ranked second when they entertained the no. 5 Wolverines. Michigan erased a 10-point first-half lead, but Illinois rebuilt its advantage to 13 in the second half. Michigan rallied within 78–74 but drew no closer.

Michigan routed no. 18 Ohio State in the fourth Big Ten game, which marked Vaught's return to the starting five, where he'd remain for all but one game the rest of the season. Vaught also succeeded Rice as Michigan's leading rebounder that season, averaging eight boards per game.

Vaught "was probably as skilled as far as rebounding the ball as anyone I've played with," Hughes says. "He just went and got it. Some guys may be more athletic, some guys may be longer, but he just had a knack for rebounding the ball."

There were several key emotional moments for Michigan in 1988–89, but Wisconsin was an unlikely spot for the first one, as the host Badgers entered the contest just 1-4 in Big Ten play. But with nine seconds remaining and Wisconsin leading 69–68, Robinson missed two free throws, and the Badgers emerged with a 71–68 victory.

After the game, Rice says, he "went right up to him, I said, 'Rumeal, do we wish you had hit the free throws? Absolutely. But don't worry about it. You're going to get a chance again.'" Little did Rice know how accurate his prediction would be.

Robinson began preparing for that hoped-for second chance immediately, by coming early to practice and shooting at least 100 extra free throws every day for the next two weeks. "I remember [Robinson] saying, 'That'll never happen to me again,'" Mills says.

After the Wisconsin loss, the 10th-ranked Wolverines returned home to face 16th-ranked Indiana. U-M held a 54–50 advantage midway through the second half when Robinson's foul trouble helped open things up for Indiana's Jay Edwards, who scored 20 of his 28 points after the break.

Indiana led for most of the closing minutes, but Michigan had the final possession, trailing 71–70. What followed was a scenario that would be repeated—almost exactly—in the NCAA tournament about 10 weeks later. With primary options Rice and Higgins defended too closely, Mills launched a 3-pointer from the corner that missed. Hughes rebounded the shot on the baseline and put it back up, but the ball glanced off the rim to end the game. Michigan fell to 3-3 in conference play, three games behind 6-0 Indiana.

"I know that people were unhappy," Frieder says. "The media was criticizing us. And yet, I was not upset.…I knew in my own mind we were just a couple of plays away from being 5-1 instead of 3-3."

Part of Michigan's early-season problems, Hughes says, were "a couple of issues" that he, as captain, decided to handle. "Sean would get a little shot-happy at times. So would Rumeal. So these are guys I'd have to corral and have a little tête-à-tête and say, 'Hey, man, look. Let's move the ball.' Or, 'Hey, Glen hasn't touched the ball in the last four minutes,' or, 'Get the ball to Terry inside.' Whatever the case may be."

Vaught recalls that early in the conference season, some players also lacked a bit of focus. "I thought that, at times, there were some distractions with some of our more high-profile guys maybe being a little distracted by talk of coming out of school, or agents saying things, and reading scouting reports about your pro prospects."

The Indiana game also marked the end of U-M's lineup shuffling. After that contest, Mills, Rice, Vaught, Robinson and Griffin started virtually every game, with Hughes, Higgins and, for the moment, guard Kirk Taylor

Bill Frieder is third
in career victories
among U-M
basketball coaches.
*BL016950, Bentley
Historical Library,
University of
Michigan.*

as the first players off the bench. The key decision was to start the defensive-minded Griffin rather than the shooting ace Higgins, although Higgins still played around 20 minutes per game.

"Sean Higgins was a great player," Frieder says. "Sean probably didn't have quite the work ethic that, say, a Glen Rice did, or a Rumeal Robinson, or a Gary Grant, earlier. So I probably was a little harder on him than others because I thought he should be better than what he was doing. So he might've deserved to start, talent-wise, and yet I brought him off the bench to keep him hungry."

The Wolverines bounced back with victories over Purdue and Michigan State before traveling to pre-season no. 1–ranked Iowa. The Hawkeyes hadn't quite matched their high expectations but were still 17-4 overall, 5-3 in the Big Ten—tied with Michigan—and ranked no. 8. Fifty minutes later, Michigan gained its biggest victory since defeating Oklahoma, edging Iowa in double overtime, 108–107. The Hawkeyes erased a 21-point deficit to take the lead late in regulation time, before a Mills put-back at the buzzer sent the game into OT, 83–83. Higgins hit three straight triples to keep U-M alive in the first overtime and then fed Vaught for the winning hoop in the second OT.

Meanwhile, in early February, Arizona State head coach Steve Patterson announced his resignation. Just before the Michigan-Iowa game, the *Arizona Republic* printed a list of ten coaches thought to be candidates for the vacancy. Frieder's name was on the list.

Heartbreak and Renewal in Bloomington

Two days after beating Iowa, U-M dropped an 88–80 decision at Minnesota. Additionally, Michigan's backcourt depth took a hit as Taylor suffered a season-ending knee injury. Taylor had become a key role player, seeing at least 21 minutes of action in each of the previous three games, while contributing a solid five assists and four points per contest. "It was a huge loss for us at the time," Frieder says, "because…he was a quick guard who could defend and make things happen—make plays and get you into your offense."

After defeating Purdue again, Michigan traveled to no. 13 Indiana for the next emotional turning point of the season. Michigan trailed 42–37 at halftime but had a larger problem. Rice was ill, fighting the flu and bronchitis. He ended up scoring just seven points in the game, shooting 2-for-10, and missed about 10 minutes of the second half with four fouls.

Still, Michigan led 75–73 with 54 seconds remaining. U-M ran the clock down almost to the end before feeding Rice down low. Rice, a bit off balance, missed the potential game-clinching shot off the glass. Indiana rebounded, cleared half-court and got the ball to Jay Edwards by the top of the key. Edwards released the ball as, or perhaps slightly after, the clock struck zero (there was no video review rule in 1989), but a fraction of a second before the buzzer sounded. His 3-point shot dropped through the hoop to give the Hoosiers a 76–75 victory, their second 1-point win over Michigan in less than a month.

After the game, the public question was whether Edwards's shot was released in time. But a more important story played out in the visitors' locker room, where the emotional seeds of Michigan's upcoming NCAA run were planted. "It didn't sit well with us, losing to Indiana at that time, especially at the buzzer," Rice says. "We didn't blame anybody but ourselves because we didn't feel like we came out and played the way we were capable.…I remember us having some bickering and guys—I wouldn't say fighting—but arguing and telling one another to man up on their mistakes."

Rice says the criticism was "very constructive" and was accepted "because of the respect we had for one another." But the squad also needed some positive reinforcement. Frieder offered the first dose and spoke one of the words that came to represent Michigan's quest for the remainder of the season. Frieder says he "talked to my team a long time, much longer than I normally did after games. Told them how proud I was of them, how good they were, and [that] we're going to be on a mission to win the national championship, because we're a team capable of doing so."

Rice, who usually preferred to lead by actions, then expanded on Frieder's "mission" theme in a brief but memorable speech, words that resonated with his teammates for the rest of the season. Rice said he was "tired of games going this way," as Mills recalls. Rice declared that Michigan wouldn't lose again, that the team was on "a mission. A mission to shock the world."

"It just came to me," Rice says. "It just felt like it was the right time to say something. I never was the one to get up and say anything. But I just felt at that time that, if I didn't, then the season could easily have gone on a totally different way. And I didn't want that to happen. I could see in the guys' faces that the hurt from that game was deep. And you lose a game like that sometimes, and it could go either way. It could be an unsuccessful season from that point on, or it could be a very good one. It just depends on the mindset and the approach that guys take after that game. And I wanted to make sure that we took the right approach and we realized that, OK, just because of this one loss, not to let us be discouraged and lose sight of the goals that we had.…It was not the time to sit there and be quiet and hope that everyone understood what had to be done."

The phrase "shock the world," oft-repeated since that day—including once by Juwan Howard during the 1992 NCAA tournament—"just came out of my mouth," Rice recalls, "just like that. 'Let's shock the world. We're on a mission to shock the world.' Because people probably were giving us a long shot to win it.…And it just fit in, because it was not scripted."

Rice's normally more talkative co-captain, Hughes, says Rice's speech "sparked us.…I think guys understood, and we all started playing the way we're supposed to play. Making the extra pass. Making sure you communicate on defense. You switch when you're supposed to. We're boxing out. Doing the things we were supposed to do to win games."

Heating Up

Part of the reason the Wolverines turned their focus to the NCAA tournament was the obvious fact that they were out of the Big Ten race. U-M was 7-5, while Indiana was 11-1 and on its way to the conference championship. Nevertheless, Michigan took care of business in its remaining Big Ten contests, with one exception.

"It seemed like the light bulb came on at that point," Vaught says, "and we all put the little petty jealousies aside and embraced all of our individual roles and didn't concern ourselves with, 'This guy's scoring more than me or shooting more than me.'"

Michigan played its final regular-season game at home, the traditional Senior Night, against no. 4 Illinois. U-M was hot, but the Illini had their star, Kendall Gill, back from an injury and were halfway through what became a 10-game winning streak. Gill entered the contest with the score 17–17 but soon triggered an 18–4 run from which Michigan never recovered in a stinging 89–73 defeat.

Prior to the game, "I was very excited," Hughes says. "I mean, your parents are there, everything's going well, it's great. We're fired up....Man, next thing you know, these guys are flying all over, dunking stuff in."

Mills calls the defeat "quite embarrassing, and we still talk about that today." But in another prophetic moment in Michigan's magic season, Mills promised his teammates that they hadn't seen the last of the Illini. "I said we should get another shot at them in the tournament."

The Wolverines won five of their last six conference games, to finish third in the Big Ten at 12-6. Overall, Frieder says, "We were really playing well right then....This was a team that was in the regionals the year before, and now they're starting to peak and come on and play real well at the right time, heading into the tournament. So I really liked our chances."

What Frieder didn't know was that he'd coached his final game at Michigan.

FRIEDER EXITS WITHOUT FLOURISHES

The Arizona State coaching story simmered in the background throughout February and into March, during which time Frieder wouldn't discuss it publicly. Hughes remembers hearing rumors of Frieder leaving, "but nobody thought he'd do it. We were like, 'Oh yeah, that's just talk.'"

Behind the scenes, however, Arizona State athletic director Charles Harris, a former assistant AD at Michigan in the '70s, had contacted U-M and obtained permission to speak with Frieder around the beginning of March. Harris eventually offered the ASU job to Frieder and insisted on a quick decision. Three days after losing to Illinois, just a few hours after a U-M practice and three days before Michigan opened NCAA play, Frieder and his wife, Janice, flew to Arizona to finalize the deal. Like Orr in 1980, Frieder would receive a multi-year written contract—he'd still been working on one-year handshake deals at U-M—that gave Frieder the security he desired.

Frieder says that he and his wife "always wanted to go out west. I got a great job offer, and just felt it was time to leave Michigan. I didn't like the football coach being the athletic director. I didn't think basketball was getting all the things that it needed. I think there were a lot of unhappy people in Ann Arbor because they felt that we underachieved a little.."

Schembechler, quoted after Frieder's departure in the 1989 book *Mission Accomplished!*, said of Frieder, "I never had any problem with him. But I think he anticipated he would have problems with me, and that's what prompted all this. And probably, he was right."

Despite his attempt to keep the meeting secret, word of Frieder's trip to Arizona leaked, so he began phoning his players, still believing that he would coach them in the tournament. "The conversation probably lasted about a half hour," Mills recalls, "and he was just basically saying that he hasn't given up on us, but you know this is something that he has to do. He just said that it's about his family."

In a 1999 interview in the *Wolverine* magazine, Canham recalled speaking to Frieder about the Arizona State job. Canham advised Frieder that if he accepted the position, "'Bo's going to broom you out of there.' He said, 'Naw, he wouldn't do that until after the tournament.'…The relationship between Bo and Frieder was never very good. They were just different personalities."

Frieder says that he couldn't reach Schembechler by phone regarding his decision but spoke with assistant athletic director Jack Weidenbach Wednesday morning, two days before Michigan's first NCAA game. "I finally got ahold of Jack and told him I was taking the Arizona State job at the end of the season, and it was going to get announced.…Weidenbach called me back and said he didn't think Bo was going to let me coach the team. Then obviously, the rest, as they say, is history. I did finally talk to Bo—when he told me [that Frieder couldn't coach in the NCAA tournament], I said, 'Well, I don't agree with you, Bo, but I respect your decision.' And I says, 'You've got a quality man to run the team for us, and that's Steve Fisher.' And that was it."

Shortly thereafter, Schembechler spoke to the media. "I don't want someone from Arizona State coaching the Michigan team," Schembechler said. "I want that understood. A Michigan man is going to coach Michigan."

Speaking during a Big Ten Network documentary of the 1988–89 season, Fisher said he was shocked when he learned that he'd be taking the coaching reins from Frieder. "I could've been knocked over with a feather," Fisher said. "You don't not let a guy coach on the eve of a tournament. You don't fire a coach, hire an interim coach, right before you go to the NCAA tournament."

Rice says the team would've accepted Frieder as their coach during the tournament. "Bill Frieder had brought us through so much and had been there so many times for us," Rice says. "We were like, fine, if that's what you want to do, that's fine. We want you to be our coach. You brought us up this far. So let's do this. We understood what was going on. Bill was not looked upon as an outsider to us. That was our coach. That was our friend. And that was our father. He was there with us. It was his team. It pisses me off that he doesn't get any credit that he deserves."

BO RALLIES THE TROOPS

Things were happening fast in Ann Arbor. One week earlier, the team was on a roll, playing its best basketball of the season. The Wolverines then suffered back-to-back body blows with an embarrassing defeat to Illinois and the loss of their head coach. Their recovery began when Schembechler met with the team and delivered the type of pep talk normally heard in the Big House next door, not in Crisler Arena. He began by explaining his decision to replace Frieder with Fisher.

"He didn't believe it was right for a guy to have another job and finish out coaching as a lame duck," Vaught says. Schembechler also emphasized that, although others may have written off Michigan's season, he had full confidence in the team. "And somehow or another, the guy just has a way with his words, his inflection—when he's loud, when he's quiet. When he looks you in the eye. When he turns his back and [paces]. I mean, the guy was an excellent communicator/motivator. And at the end of the meeting, we almost felt better off, that everybody had jumped off our bandwagon."

"That, 'til this day, probably was the best motivational speech I have ever heard," Rice says. "He had us believing that we could take off our dirty socks and walk up to somebody and tell 'em, 'These socks are brand-new,' and make a sale. That's how he had us believing. And what I respect the most about that is, he not once said a bad word about Frieder."

Schembechler spoke to the team at Fisher's request. But Schembechler, who hadn't appreciated reading published comments in which Higgins mentioned the possibility of transferring, warned Fisher that speaking to the team might be counterproductive.

In the book *Bo's Lasting Lessons*, Schembechler said, "So I asked Fisher, 'Are you sure you want me to talk to your team? Because you might be without one or two players in that room when I'm done.'" Fisher didn't back away from his request, and Schembechler issued challenges that the players have never forgotten.

After Schembechler's motivational words, Mills says, "It was time for him to lay it out there on the line. And I think he might have started off with Sean Higgins, and he said, 'Higgins, you know what? I'm so tired of hearing this shit about you wanting to transfer and you wanting to get out of here.' I can remember him reaching in his back pocket and pulling out [some papers], and he said, 'I got these [transfer] papers right here,' he said, 'now what the hell do you want to do?' And everybody was kind of in awe and like, what the hell? And the next thing you know, it was my turn, and it was like, 'Terry Mills, I'm so tired of hearing shit about what you're supposed to do and what kind of man you're supposed to be, and I'm tired of hearing this and that.' And he just went right down the line and everybody was kind of like in awe. Because I was always one of these guys that, I would challenge a coach, I would stand up to a coach. And once he got to me and once he ripped into me, my teammates, they stood there and looked at me like, 'Whoa, aren't you gonna do something, aren't you gonna say something?' And I'm frozen, like, 'Man, are you kidding me? This guy just ripped into me.'

"Once he left out of there, it was just total silence, and we just went to practice after that. And we joked about it after practice, it was like, 'Yeah, you didn't do nothing, you didn't stand up.' 'Well, Higgins, what did you do, why didn't you go get the papers, you've been talking about transferring?'…I think Bo basically had lit a fire under us."

Frieder, meanwhile, left with a 191–87 record and two Big Ten championships, plus an NIT title. But some observers were dissatisfied due to Michigan's perceived failures in recent NCAA tournaments and because of the timing of his exit.

"Regarding the [ASU] job," Frieder says, "obviously if I had it to do over again I'd do it differently. I guess there's two main points. One, I should've never put myself in that position during the season. So that one was on me. But probably where I made a mistake is, I shouldn't have been truthful. Because all I had to do to go to Atlanta [for the NCAA tournament] was say, 'I'm not going to discuss jobs.'…But I decided, when word was leaking out that I would go to Arizona State at the end of the season, I decided to be honest and up front. So that cost me coaching my team."

And that left the Wolverines with the key question: Was Frieder right about Steve Fisher? At the most important time of the season, did Michigan have a quality man to run the team?

REDEMPTION AND REWARD, 1989

The 10th-ranked Wolverines, 24-7 overall, drew a third seed in the Southeast Regional and left Ann Arbor with Schembechler's words still echoing in their ears. But the players hadn't heard their last speech of the day. There to greet them in Atlanta was their now ex-coach, Frieder.

"That was very emotional for me….because these kids, they did a lot for me," Frieder says. "They believed in Bill Frieder, they came to Michigan, they played hard for me, they won a lot of basketball games….It was very tough, but I wished them the very best. I says, 'Remember what our goal was, to win the national championship. Go out and get it done.'"

The players had mixed reactions to Frieder's talk. "It was sad," Vaught recalls. "He was remorseful. He didn't anticipate not being able to finish out the year, and he wished that he was allowed to. But going forward, he wished us all well….He seemed like he was kind of torn, like he wanted to be a part of that same old group. But he also had to be optimistic about his future going forward at ASU as well. It was funky. It was a weird meeting. No one knew how to really act around him. Is he a traitor? Did he get the short end of the stick? We were kind of wondering, 'How did we feel about this?'"

STEVE FISHER

The new interim head coach, Steve Fisher, had been a three-year basketball player and then graduate assistant at Illinois State, a high school head coach and then a college assistant at Western Michigan before coming to U-M. He had never been a college head coach.

Fortunately for Fisher and his team, Frieder had followed Orr's example and given his assistants plenty of responsibility. "The way Bill Frieder ran his program, he was a master delegator," Fisher told the *Sporting News* a few years later. "So I was very involved in everything about the program. Not many assistant coaches have the luxury to do those things. At times, he would have me plan practice or run practice while he would sit back and observe. I would always give the initial pregame talk to the team. So it wasn't as if I was the silent guy on the side that never said anything except, 'Good job.' He gave me the privilege and freedom to do things that allowed that transition to be a little easier than it could have or should have been."

The players may have had a variety of emotions regarding Frieder's departure, but they clearly entered the tournament united by an "us against them" attitude. From the outside, all eyes were on Fisher, waiting to see whether the players would accept him. From the inside, however, there was no question about responding to Fisher's leadership. But on the eve of the tournament, Fisher made sure he had his key player's full support.

"I remember Steve Fisher coming to me and saying, 'Glen, you know… I'm new at this, I'm just going to ask for your help,'" Rice says. "'It's a transition for us all. We are not going to do anything different. You guys go out there and play hard. If you help me, I'm going to help you. And let's go win this thing.' And let me tell you, Steve Fisher, he had those little rosy cheeks, and how could you not go out there and lay it all on the line for a great guy like him?"

In addition to their desire to win a championship, and to prove their doubters wrong, the Wolverines now had still more motivation: to win for Steve Fisher.

Fencing with the Musketeers

Michigan's first opponent, the 14th-seeded Xavier Musketeers, entered the NCAA tournament 21-11 after placing third in the Midwestern City Conference. The game began shakily as Michigan committed 11 first-half turnovers against the Musketeers' pressure defense and trailed 45–42 at the break. Reserve Demetrius Calip committed three of those turnovers when he spelled Robinson briefly at point guard.

For a while, the contest looked like a familiar Michigan first-round NCAA game in which U-M would muddle through unimpressively. But with 9:35 left, Xavier still held a 71–65 lead. No doubt the "Coaching Change Kills Michigan" story was already being typed as the upset loomed.

At that point, Fisher put Calip back onto the court. In a performance reminiscent of "Tournament Tom" Staton, Calip promptly drove to the hoop, was fouled as he scored and completed the 3-point play. Shortly thereafter, a Calip put-back pulled U-M within 74–73 with 6:08 left.

Rice, who'd scored 13 points in the first half before cooling off, then heated back up with a pair of triples that put Michigan on top, 84–82. Calip remained hot, sinking a jumper with about three minutes remaining to increase the lead to 86–83. The reserve guard also hit a pair of free throws in the final minute, as the Wolverines survived with a 92–87 victory.

But Michigan might not have won if Fisher hadn't given Calip a second chance. Calip sat below Kirk Taylor on the depth chart early in the season and played a total of 14 minutes in Michigan's first 10 conference games. After Taylor's injury, Calip averaged 11 minutes per game in the remaining conference contests. He finished with nine points in 14 minutes against Xavier, with no turnovers in the second half. He also played well defensively.

Indeed, Hughes says that Michigan's comeback against Xavier began on the defensive end. "We ended up finally getting some stops," Hughes says. "I thought they played more free in the first half; they were able to do what they wanted to do. They ran their stuff. And I think the second half we were able to adjust."

Offensively, Rice and Robinson led Michigan with 23 points apiece. It would be Rice's lowest point total of the tourney. As a team, Rice says Michigan might have been "so amped up, so excited, that we allowed ourselves to play somewhat to their level. At times we would take quick shots. Defensive rotations weren't up to par, like they had been....We were so ready to get that thing going that we sputtered a little bit when we came out of the gate."

Another Close Call

Michigan faced Sun Belt Conference tournament champion South Alabama in the second round. The 23-8 Jaguars, seeded 11th, had upset 6th-seeded Alabama, thanks mainly to a quick backcourt led by Junie "Peanut Butter" Lewis and Jeff "Jelly" Hodge. But as the game began, it wasn't the food-themed backcourt that upset the Wolverines' stomachs as much as the referees' whistles. Michigan committed 17 first-half fouls, which the Jaguars converted into 15 points at the free-throw line—while only committing five fouls themselves—on the way to a 47–44 lead at the break.

At halftime, Fisher told the Wolverines to forget about the officiating. "He told us, 'You guys are doing too much bitching and whining,'" Hughes said after the game. "You worry about playing basketball and let me take care of the other stuff."

The Jaguars led by six early in the second half, but Michigan rallied for a 67–67 tie with 12:20 remaining. It was still 80-all with 2:40 left when the Wolverines finally gained some breathing room. A Mills 3-point play off a turnaround jumper with 2:17 left was almost immediately followed by a Rice 3-point basket to make it 86–80. U-M then hung on for a 91–82 victory.

Rice led Michigan in scoring—as he did in each tournament game—with 36 points on 16-for-25 shooting. And, as he would do so often over the next few weeks, Rice scored when it counted the most. He tallied 11 of Michigan's 17 points in one stretch as the Wolverines pushed a 1-point edge to a 6-point lead with two minutes remaining. Additionally, with Robinson carrying four personals, Rice guarded the 6-foot-3 Lewis, who'd been posting up the 6-1 Calip. "We looked past them," Rice says, "just a little bit….They, more so than Xavier, gave us a wake-up call."

Hughes, who started the game in Vaught's usual spot, says the Jaguars "played hard," adding that the Wolverines prevailed due to better talent, "and our size kind of got 'em in the end, with second shots, put-backs, things like that." Indeed, South Alabama didn't have an answer for Mills, who scored 24 points on 9-for-13 shooting, with seven rebounds.

Despite a second straight close call, Michigan's post-game locker room was upbeat, with Fisher setting the example. "Nothing he says is negative," Robinson said after the contest. "Everything is positive; positive thinking, which is probably the greatest thing you can have in basketball."

In some ways, Vaught adds, Fisher "was like Frieder's opposite. Where Bill Frieder was very frenzied and he looked a little out of control, he looked a little wild sometimes on the sidelines, disheveled, Fisher, he was a different personality. He was kind of an educator. He would talk to you, look you in the eye, he would talk to you quietly and calmly. He'd make sure everybody understood, everybody was on the same page."

While many would make the Frieder-versus-Fisher comparison during Michigan's tournament run, assistant coach Brian Dutcher noted that Fisher's exact words might've been less important than the new voice that was speaking them. "You go to class every day and hear the same teacher," Dutcher told *Sports Illustrated*. "Then one day you get a guest lecturer, and what he says seems fresh. Steve wasn't doing anything much different, but the freshness came at the right time."

BEATING THE BULLY

Despite the unexpected coaching change, Michigan's tournament performance to this point was little different from the previous years, with two closer-than-expected victories over lesser teams. And now U-M would face its familiar postseason roadblock: 2nd-seeded, 29-7 North Carolina. If they continued to follow their usual script, the Wolverines' season was about to end. This, of course, is where the 1989 team's path diverged from its predecessors'.

The change began in the players' minds. One year earlier, Rice had felt that Michigan wasn't ready for North Carolina. Now, he says, the Wolverines were "begging for that game.…We were not going to lose. I wasn't ever worried about losing to them. There was no way in the world a team was going to beat us three times. Not me being a part of it. I have great respect for their team, great respect for their coach. But we were not coming out of that game as losers."

Hughes says the players felt the matchup with 5th-ranked North Carolina was "payback time. It's time to overcome the bully."

To prepare for the schools' third straight NCAA matchup, Fisher and his staff put together a 15-minute film from the previous year's game. But rather than show his players what they did wrong, Fisher played the positive card again. The film contained only U-M highlights, to show the team what was possible.

Vaught returned to the starting lineup for the regional semifinal, played in Lexington, Kentucky. The first half was a shootout, largely between Rice and Carolina guard Jeff Lebo, who sank consecutive triples to give the Tar Heels a 26–18 lead 7:12 into the game. A Rice 3-pointer helped Michigan battle back, while a Mills layup followed by a fast-break Rice dunk late in the half made it 50–47 U-M at the break.

The teams combined to sink 13 triples in the first half, with Lebo hitting five and Rice four. The difference was that Rice kept hitting them in the second half and Lebo didn't. After scoring 17 points in the first 20 minutes, Lebo connected on just two free throws in the second half.

Glen Rice was Michigan's hottest shooter during the 1989 NCAA tournament. *BL008106, Bentley Historical Library, University of Michigan.*

Nevertheless, it was a battle to the final minute. Back-to-back triples by Rice and Robinson gave U-M a 62–61 edge with about 12 minutes left. North Carolina never led again, but U-M didn't pull far away either. The Wolverines built the lead as high as 71–64 before the Tar Heels rallied within one. But that was Rice's cue. His 3-pointer with 5:53 remaining made it 79–75. Once more North Carolina responded, tying the contest at 83 with 4:07 remaining. Michigan edged in front again, and then Rice hit the dagger, a triple from the corner that gave Michigan a 90–85 lead with 1:02 on the clock.

"They had a missed assignment....They had a defensive breakdown," Rice recalls, "and we were already moving. And at that point in time I don't understand how you let a guy like myself even get open, even for half a second. Because most of the time that's all it took."

North Carolina's J.R. Reid answered with a basket and then got another chance after Robinson missed the front end of a 1-and-1. But Reid missed a shot, Higgins rebounded and was fouled. He then sank both free throws with 27 seconds left to provide the final margin in a 92–87 victory.

"I think it was a great thing that North Carolina was in our way," Rice says, "because they made sure we kept that extra edge that we needed. I think if we'd have had a lesser-caliber team—maybe a team that we hadn't faced in the previous two tournaments, and knocked us out—we probably would've won, but maybe we wouldn't have looked at that team the same way. We looked at [North Carolina] with red eyes. We had to beat them."

Rice shot 13-for-19 overall and was 8-for-12 from 3-point range for 34 points, including 11 points in the final six minutes. Higgins played his best tournament game to date, scoring 14 points and dishing out three assists in 21 minutes, while Robinson finished with 17 points plus 13 assists.

Additionally, Hughes says, North Carolina "didn't get a whole lot of easy baskets." In the teams' previous meetings, he adds, "they got that ball inside easy and got easy looks. But [in 1989], we were able to offset that a little bit, force them to take jumpers, and we'd rebound the ball."

With the huge victory in their pocket, "Our excitement is building," Vaught recalls. "We're starting to wrap our heads around the possibility that we have a great chance here."

Routing Virginia

Michigan's regional final opponent, unranked Virginia, was seeded fifth and entered tournament play with an unspectacular 19-10 record but had just upset top-seeded Oklahoma.

Rice says Michigan simultaneously took Virginia seriously and remained confident of victory. "We thought that they didn't belong on the court with us," Rice says. "And one thing we wanted to do was, get rid of them fast. Deliver a blow that they could not bounce back from. Because we didn't want to be one of those, 'Oh my God it was a great team but they underestimated or looked past [another] team.' We weren't going to have that."

The game went according to Rice's script, as Michigan rolled to a 44–25 halftime lead. Virginia tried a variety of defenses, including a box-and-one that keyed on Rice, but couldn't slow him down. Higgins elevated his game in the second half, nailing six consecutive triples on his way to 31 points, shooting 11-for-15 overall, 7-for-10 from 3-point range. And he succeeded on both ends of the floor, teaming with Griffin to limit Virginia's leading scorer, Richard Morgan, to 15 points on 5-for-18 shooting.

Rice finished with 32 points on 13-for-16 shooting overall, 4-for-5 from beyond the arc. When the final triple had dropped, Michigan was the regional champion with a 102–65 blowout victory.

The 37-point margin "was not a surprise," Rice says. "Because at that time we already understood how to prepare ourselves for the next game," so there was no letdown after the emotional victory over North Carolina.

When the players cut down the nets before leaving the Lexington floor, they left the final strand for Fisher. After four games, the players remained solidly supportive of the new coach, but for different reasons. Fisher "redefined our roles," Vaught says. "A lot of guys that were supposed to be distributing the ball, pushing the ball, they started getting hung up on maybe scoring. Fisher came in and tightened it all back up. If you were asked to rebound and run the floor and play D, then there was no more taking four or five ill-advised shots throughout the game. If you did, you came out."

While Fisher didn't change Michigan's basic approach, every coach handles his team differently, and some of those differences with Frieder emerged during the tournament. "I just think that he put his own seal on the personnel," Hughes says. "Some guys would play a little longer. I know Rumeal was one of Coach Frieder's favorites as far as staying on the court. And I think Coach Fisher kind of backed up on him a little bit….Put guys in different spots, gave Higgins, I think, a few more minutes. But set-wise I don't recall him really changing a whole lot on what we ran all year."

"If you've got a car that's running well, you let it run," Boyd adds. "There weren't any major changes; there was a little tweak here or tweak there."

One change that wouldn't have occurred under Frieder was Schembechler's presence as motivator-in-chief. His first speech went over so well that Fisher kept asking for encores. And Schembechler kept delivering.

"Every time Bo addressed our team," Vaught says, "when he walked out, we all would be smiling and feeling like we wanted to fight, we wanted to battle….Like, OK, that's it, that's exactly the recipe that we needed. Bo had a way of making you feel like, 'I'm about to give you what you need to know to take your ass out there and win this game.'…And you'd be feeling like that in your own heart, and then you'd look to your left and your right and you'd see that same kind of glazed-over look in your teammates' eyes also, letting you know, like, 'OK, it's not just me.'" Vaught recalls that Rice

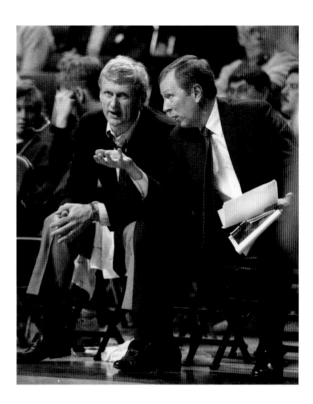

Steve Fisher (right) succeeded Bill Frieder as Michigan's head coach much sooner than either man expected. *BL010720, Bentley Historical Library, University of Michigan.*

was particularly enthusiastic about the pep talks. "Bo would leave the room, Glen would stand up and be like, 'Yeah!' Making loud shouts and hitting his chest, hitting his heart. 'That's what I'm talking about there, yeah!'"

Heavyweight Fight

After beating Virginia, Michigan awaited the winner of the Midwest Regional final between Illinois and Syracuse. While congratulating the victorious Wolverines in Lexington, Schembechler told the team, "I hope you get Illinois." Through a series of mistakes and miscommunications, a videotape of Schembechler's words went public. Once it hit the airwaves, the clip became the 1989 equivalent of a YouTube video going viral. After beating Syracuse, Illinois coach Lou Henson made a copy of the tape to show his team but told the media he might need another one because "we're going to wear the first one out."

Illinois was the only no. 1 seed to reach the Final Four in 1989. Duke was a second seed, while Michigan and Seton Hall were third seeds. The Illini were ranked third nationally with a 31-4 record, although all four losses occurred when Kendall Gill was injured, and he was now fully healthy.

Frieder, who didn't go to Lexington, did travel to Seattle for the Final Four. He thought about sneaking into the Kingdome before tip-off but ended up watching the games at his hotel. But first he met with Fisher before the Illinois game.

"He said, 'Well, Coach, what do we have to do?'" Frieder recalls. "I says, 'Hey, Coach, don't even ask. Just do what you've been doing.'" Frieder also addressed the players as a group for the last time, briefly, to offer encouragement. Although at that point, with the Illini next on Michigan's agenda, extra motivation wasn't necessary.

Rice says the players were "super-excited. We were saying to ourselves, the winner of this game is going to win the NCAA championship. At the same time, we were saying, 'Guys, remember this team came into our building, on Senior Night, and embarrassed the hell out of us. Remember.' We felt they were cocky as hell, knew they were going to walk all over us. Well, I don't think they realized what kind of mission we were on."

Mills believes the coaches had developed a solid game plan for Illinois—even in the regular season—which the team hadn't executed properly. But after two double-digit losses to the Illini in the Big Ten season, the players were ready to listen.

"The coaching staff would always say that [Illinois] had a bunch of athletic guys, and we didn't want to get involved in this track meet, up-and-down type of thing," Mills explains. "We wanted to kind of control it, use our big guys, let's bang 'em inside, let's use what we've got to our advantage. And that's something we didn't do when we played Illinois at home.…You can't tell athletes that you can't run with this team…we're not geared like that. 'Oh we can't? Yeah we will!' But then when you get jumped on and beat up then it's a whole different thing."

Hughes says Fisher "did such a tremendous job" preparing for Illinois, telling the Wolverines to "cut down turnovers [and] rebound the basketball. Keep 'em off the glass and we'll win the game." While Hughes respected Illinois' athleticism, "They didn't have a lot of great jump shooters. Kendall Gill could shoot it, Nick Anderson was a decent shooter. But the rest of 'em, they wanted to dribble-drive, they wanted to get inside.…So we turned those guys into jump shooters."

Illinois led early, 16–8, but the margin was never that large again. Michigan settled down and took a 39–38 edge into halftime and then gained its largest lead, 53–46, early in the second half, before Illinois came back. Higgins later compared the latter part of the game to a championship boxing match, with the teams exchanging body blows and neither side giving an inch.

The game featured 33 lead changes and seven ties. Eleven of those lead changes occurred in the last 8:30, as the teams combined to score on 21 of 30 possessions.

With the score tied at 74, Robinson pushed the ball upcourt and fed Hughes for a dunk. Robinson then stole an Illinois pass and dished the ball to Rice for another slam and a 78–74 Michigan lead. Kenny Battle answered with a triple from the right side, and then Lowell Hamilton scored on a baseline jumper to give the Illini a 1-point edge with 1:36 left. With 1:09 on the clock, Mills missed a shot, but Hughes put it back up, was fouled and hit the free throw for an 81–79 lead.

Battle responded to Hughes's 3-point play by hitting a mid-range jumper with 30 seconds remaining. Prior to Battle's basket, Fisher told his team he wouldn't call a timeout after Illinois' possession but would "let you guys win it." If Illinois scored, however, he wanted either Rice or Higgins to work open off screens and take the last shot.

Now, with the score 81–81, the quick Illini stayed with Rice and Higgins, Michigan's deadly shooting aces. With time running down, Robinson dribbled to the left side, down to the baseline and then flung a pass to Mills in the far-right corner—the same spot from which he missed in the first Indiana game—with about five seconds on the clock.

"We were trying to get Glen the ball because Glen had a hot hand," Mills recalls. "And somehow we just could not get him the ball, it didn't work out that way, and basically ended up with me with the ball in my hands. And…I remember the bench saying, 'You gotta shoot it!' And I took that shot, and I remember it coming off, and then I remember it's like, it was complete silence."

Mills's 3-point attempt flew straight but a bit short, hit the front rim and bounced over the basket along the baseline. Nick Anderson had the inside position to grab the rebound, but Higgins was quicker. While Mills was shooting, Higgins had moved into the best possible rebounding spot, right behind Anderson. Higgins then timed his jump perfectly and snared the ball, just as Hughes had rebounded Mills's miss against the Hoosiers in January. But this time, Higgins's put-back fell softly through the hoop. Rice then caught Illinois' desperation inbounds pass, giving Michigan an 83–81 victory and a spot in the national final.

"Higgins did a great job of sliding in on the weak side, where a lot of times people stand and watch," Boyd says. Higgins credited Fisher, saying after the game that the former assistant "has been telling me all year that shots like that come off the weak side, so I put myself in position for the rebound."

"The ball went over [Anderson's] head," Higgins told reporters. "He didn't see me coming because his head was turned until he had me on his back. He had his body on me, but he didn't really have me totally boxed out."

Overall, Rice believes that Michigan played tougher than it had in its two previous games with Illinois. "I don't think we allowed them to run as much as we did when they came and whupped us" earlier in the season, Rice says. "We delivered blow for blow with them. And I don't think to that point that they had many teams do that. Especially a team that they just rolled over. So they were shocked. They couldn't understand why we were still there and we were the one throwing most of the punches."

After beating Illinois, "We talked about being a team of destiny," Fisher later told the Big Ten Network, "being a team that accomplished something that had never happened in the storied history of Michigan basketball, and that was to win a national championship. And we've got one more step to go."

THE SUMMIT

Having reached the final, Hughes says the Wolverines' mantra was to avoid being satisfied just to be there. "We made it to the championship game, but that's not enough," Hughes says. "Because I remember, I think it was Sean that was like, 'Yeah, we're in the championship game, yeah, yeah, yeah!' And I said, 'Hey, man, we're here, [but] we came to win, remember?' And we had to keep our focus. Getting to the Final Four wasn't good enough. Getting to the championship game wasn't good enough. We've got to win the game."

Michigan got its first idea of what the final might bring even before tipping off against Illinois, as Seton Hall rallied from behind to beat Duke in the first semifinal game. "We felt we should beat this team," Mills recalls, "but we also felt that, based on what we'd seen on this team against Duke, is that this team won't quit."

But Seton Hall had reasons to be concerned as well, starting with Rice's hot shooting. "I just felt good about Glen," Vaught says. "I had never seen him in that kind of a mode before, for that length of time. This guy's jump shot, for a month, he just was all net and his confidence was at an all-time high....I felt that there's no way we can lose with Glen hitting every shot he puts up."

Seton Hall entered the final 31-6, ranked 11th, just one spot below Michigan. The Pirates finished second in the Big East behind Georgetown and earned a third seed in the West Regional. They'd beaten 14th-seed Southwest Missouri State and 11th-seed Evansville and then caught everyone's attention by knocking off 2nd-seeded Indiana and 4th-seed UNLV to reach the Final Four. Down 18 about eight minutes into the national semifinal, the Pirates blew Duke out of the water in the second half to win, 95–78.

Seton Hall featured some international flair with 6-foot-7 Australian Andrew Gaze, a forward with great shooting range, and Puerto Rican Ramon Ramos, the team's power player at 6-foot-8, 250 pounds. Rounding out the lineup were 6-foot-8 forward Daryll Walker, 6-foot-3 guard John Morton—the team's leading scorer—and 6-foot-1 guard Gerald Greene, a high school opponent of Rumeal Robinson. All were seniors except Gaze, a twenty-three-year-old who'd played for Australia's Olympic team. A strong defensive team—Seton Hall had held opponents to 41.1 percent shooting entering the final—the Pirates generally played tougher as the game progressed, in part due to a deep bench.

On the afternoon of the NCAA Final, Fisher began the biggest day of his career by forgetting his credential and was stopped by a Kingdome guard before an NCAA official vouched for him. But Fisher wasn't at a loss when speaking to his team. "We played at the Kingdome, and at that time, they had all the championship banners surrounding the upper tier," Fisher later told the *Sporting News*. "And I said, 'As you go out, making your first circle around the court, look up at those banners. There are no runner-ups that are there. Let's hang our banner tonight after this game.'"

Looking back, Vaught says his emotions were focused on his teammates. "You're a kid, so you get it, but you don't get it," Vaught says. "I felt like those guys were my brothers, not my teammates anymore. Because it's like a do-or-die situation. You've been through good times, you've been through bad times. You've been through arguments, and you've been through fights in practice, cuss-out sessions and all kinds of stuff goes on that nobody ever really knows about. But if you're there with those guys, that's who you're going to war with and those are your dogs, those are your brothers at that point. And I remember just looking around the room, feeling like in some way, we're attached forever, because this is going to go down in history."

The game opened auspiciously for Michigan, with Rice sinking a jumper six seconds in. The Wolverines soon built a 20–14 lead on a Vaught put-back, followed by a Robinson hoop with 9:33 left. Then it was Seton Hall's turn, posting a 9–0 run over the next 2:36, including back-to-back Greene triples. Rice's first triple, part of a 15–4 U-M run, put the Wolverines back on top, 31–30, on their way to a 37–32 halftime advantage. Robinson, who'd been driving to the hoop effectively, had 14 points and Rice 13. Morton had 10 for Seton Hall, but Gaze, the Pirates' key outside shooter, had just two points, both from the foul line.

At halftime, Rice notes, "I remember Fisher just telling us, 'Guys, keep working at it, keep plugging away, keep trying to do the right things, stay together....They're going to make their run. They make a run, don't panic. Just relax and withstand the run, and [then] you go on one yourself. And be ready to go until the final buzzer.'"

Michigan began the second half by extending its lead, but Rice says the players tried to avoid feeling as if they were in control. "We didn't want to think that way," Rice says. "We had guys that were putting in a lot of minutes. We understood at any given time somebody could get tired and the game could change. We just tried to keep pushing forward. We saw that team play against Duke. We understood that they can lure you to sleep and tried not to fall too deep into that."

"Seton Hall was deep, well-coached, great big men, great guard play," Vaught recalls. "They were a good team. But we had pretty good control of the game [most of the way]. It got a little hairy, of course...."

Before things got hairy, Michigan's lead reached double digits. A Rice triple made it 49–37 with 16:51 left. Robinson's baseline drive and spectacular, over-the-head reverse dunk gave U-M a 51–39 lead with 14:17 remaining. But Robinson, who'd been penetrating well all night, shifted to more of a playmaking role at that point. U-M's offense then slowed and almost stopped, as Morton led the Pirates back. "In the second half," Hughes says, "we took a nice lead....We kind of relaxed just a little, and that's all it takes."

Seton Hall pulled within 53–47 on two Morton free throws midway through the half, before a Higgins triple bumped the lead back up to nine. A Rice 3-pointer boosted U-M's lead to 59–49 with 8:26 left. Then a Walker basket and six straight points by Morton pulled the Pirates within 59–57 with 6:51 remaining. It was 61–59 when Rice sank a triple for a 5-point lead at the 6:05 mark. But Morton scored three straight hoops—two off the break, the last on an end-to-end drive—giving Seton Hall its first lead of the half, 67–66, with 2:13 left.

"It seemed like we were cruising along pretty good," Mills says. "We were up 10 or 12 points, and then all of a sudden they're on the run and they're within two. And then it's tied. And then we're down two. It was just a weird game like that because you felt like you were ahead that whole game 8-10 points and then all of a sudden it's like, 'What happened?' And then you've got this guy Morton who was hitting shots like never before."

"Two things surprised us" in the final, Rice says. "One, that Gaze did not particularly shoot the ball well, and two, Johnny Morton, I had no idea he was that kind of player....But it didn't surprise me that they were going blow-for-blow with us because they had guys on that team that understood their roles, and they worked extremely hard and their big guys played hard. They weren't afraid of us. It was a championship game that you wanted to be involved in because you realized that it could go either way."

After a Walker free throw, Rice used a Vaught screen to get open and hit his final triple of the tournament—and likely his biggest—giving the Wolverines a 69–68 edge with 1:06 left. "I wasn't looking to shoot a three," Rice recalls, "but...at that point I felt that they had a little bit of a momentum over us. We were getting tired, you could see it. Guys were missing shots that we would normally hit. We were getting tired, but we just kept fighting. I remember Fisher even saying, 'C'mon guys, we need somebody to hit a big shot.'...And I just got open a little bit, shot, it went in."

After Morton shot an air ball, Higgins sank two free throws with 34 seconds left for a 3-point lead. But Morton answered with a step-back triple to tie the game at 71 with 25 seconds remaining. Michigan ran the clock down and looked for Rice, who came around a double screen and took a pass from Higgins near the top of the key. Rice pivoted, squared up and shot, but the ball bounced off the front of the rim as the clock ran out. Rice had missed a key shot for the first time in three weeks, sending the game into overtime.

Rice himself was surprised by the miss, "because I just knew that shot, out of all the shots I had, that probably was the one that felt the easiest. Loy Vaught was telling me, 'That's probably why you missed, because you let up off the throttle, you felt that it was the easiest.' I'm like, 'You know what? You're absolutely right.' Because that was probably the one time that I relaxed, because I knew it was in."

Now the Wolverines were entering overtime disappointed, after seeing their best shooter miss the potential game-winning shot. Would the team deflate emotionally, like the 1975 squad after the C.J. Kupec miss against UCLA? To avoid that outcome, Fisher, as he later put it, chose to "lighten the mood." He told the squad that a psychic friend of his had predicted Michigan would win in overtime, by one point, and that Hughes would be involved in the winning play.

"He sat us down," Hughes recalls, "and said, 'Hey, I'm telling you...' He said a psychic told him that I was going to pick the play in the overtime for us to win. So he knows we're going to win it. And so he ended up starting me in overtime."

"We were all strung out at that moment," Griffin said after the game. "When [Fisher] said that, it got us concentrating on Mark Hughes doing something great and also got us concentrating on the overtime instead of what had just happened. So I think it was kind of a calming effect. It was a weird way to go about it, but it worked."

As he did in the first half, Rice opened the overtime with a quick basket, just seven seconds into the extra session. Gaze quickly answered with the triple Seton Hall had waited for all game. After Higgins's baseline jumper put U-M up 75–74, Mills swatted away Walker's shot in the paint but was called for goaltending. A Higgins free throw tied the game at 76, but Morton hit a 3-pointer from the top of the circle for a 79–76 Seton Hall lead with 2:50 left.

Following a missed Higgins triple, the Pirates tried to run time off the clock, but they couldn't gain the key hoop to make it a two-possession game. First Morton missed a driving shot. Shortly thereafter, Greene missed the front end of a 1-and-1 with 1:17 left.

Early in the overtime, Rice says, the Pirates "were getting buckets a little too easy. Because of the fatigue setting in, we had a lot less chatter on the defensive end. So one thing we tried to do is pick that up....Our mindset was to say, 'Let's put it all on the line now because it's do-or-die.'"

Mills broke Michigan's scoring drought with a turn-around jumper with 58 seconds remaining to trim the margin to 79–78, setting up the game's final scene.

Redemption

As Seton Hall worked the clock down on its last full possession, Michigan tried to keep the ball away from Morton. "There were a lot of switches.... We were all trying to make sure that we contained Johnny Morton," Rice says. But Morton did get the ball, guarded by Rice. With the game on the line, the battle was scorer versus scorer. "My first move was to body him when he didn't have the ball, so when he did, he'd be off balance," Rice said after the game. "I just wanted to make sure I had my hand in his face."

Rice did have a hand in Morton's face when the Seton Hall star entered the paint and lofted his shot. Rice then turned quickly to the hoop as Morton's shot fell short. Rice caught the air ball with about eight seconds left and then passed to Robinson, near Seton Hall's free throw line. Robinson raced upcourt, with Hughes—the psychic's choice—trailing on the right and Higgins on the left wing. Dribbling through traffic with his left hand, Robinson crossed over at the top of the key and drove into the paint. He drew contact from his old East Coast rival Greene and then dished to Hughes—who was set up about 12 feet from the hoop—as the whistle blew. "My thought was to get to the basket as quick as possible," Robinson later told the Big Ten Network. "And I wasn't sure if the referees were going to blow the foul. Because who wants to be responsible for that?"

But referee John Clougherty, the ACC supervisor of officials, didn't hesitate to take responsibility, calling a blocking foul on Greene. Speaking to *Sports Illustrated* eighteen years later, Clougherty hedged just a bit when asked about the call, saying that he "would have liked to have had a clearer foul than the one we had. Instinctively, I thought there was a foul and I blew the whistle." However, he added, "There's a foul there."

After the game, Seton Hall coach P.J. Carlesimo didn't dispute the call, while Greene told reporters, "I think it could have gone either way. I just saw him penetrating to the hole. I just tried to cut him off on an angle. But we both collided together, and the ref called the foul. I felt that I was in good enough position to pick up the offensive foul, but the ref called a block."

"Gerald Greene, he couldn't believe that he got the foul called," Rice says. "The ref said that, 'You were riding up under him.' I remember him telling him that. And after that, no, [Greene] really didn't argue."

And what if the foul hadn't been called? "That would've been me on the cover of *Sports Illustrated* instead of Rumeal!" says Hughes, who'd been ready to shoot when the whistle blew. "I tell everybody that. Rumeal stole my thunder. Dish it off, I was right there, wide-open look. It was a two-on-one-type break, it was beautiful. Bang."

But instead of Hughes going "Bang" and hitting the winning shot, it was Robinson with a 1-and-1 free throw chance, with three seconds on the clock. Seton Hall called a timeout, and Fisher, true to form, told the team what to do when—not if—Robinson sank both shots. "Fish was just like, 'Hey, I know you're going to make these,'" Hughes says. "And then nobody else wanted to really [talk to Robinson]. You don't want to mess with a guy in that type of situation."

Probably the most-quoted stats after the game were Robinson's free throw percentages. He was shooting 65.2 percent for the season when he stepped to the line, and was 19-for-29 (65.5 percent) so far in the tournament. And everyone who followed Michigan remembered what had happened earlier in

Rumeal Robinson at the foul line in overtime of the 1989 NCAA Final. *Duane Black.*

the season. "As soon as he got up to the line, I flashed back to the Wisconsin game," Griffin said later. "Rumeal's been talking about that all year, about how someday he was going to redeem himself."

When he stepped to the line, "Morton starts laughing at me, trying to throw me off," Robinson said after the game. "I just start laughing back at him. I wasn't about to let him get at me."

Robinson "looked pretty calm," Hughes says. "Because he wasn't a great free throw shooter, by any stretch. But he looked ready to make these free throws. He looked together. I didn't see any, you know, wiping his hands or doing any nervous signs. He just kind of had a stoic look on his face. Like, 'OK, let's go do this.'"

As Robinson took the ball from the referee and bounced it at the line, numerous Michigan men were with him in spirit. Dave Strack and Johnny Orr—the coaches who'd led Michigan's first two national finalists—sat watching in the Kingdome stands.

Cazzie Russell, then coaching for the Atlanta Hawks, recalls watching the game on TV in a hotel lounge.

C.J. Kupec was among the many watching at home, in Ann Arbor.

Antoine Joubert, far from home, viewed the moment from France.

Steve Grote, on vacation in Denver, marveled that Clougherty "had the guts to make the [foul] call."

Joe Johnson, in Lansing of all places, calls the moment "the most nerve-wracking thing I could ever remember seeing."

In his California home, Gary Grant thought, "OK Rumeal, all that practicing and everything that you were doing, always talking about, you would hit 'em at the crucial [time]—here we go!"

And in his Seattle hotel room, Frieder says he "thought of the Wisconsin game and I said, 'I know he's gonna make 'em.'"

At the foul line, with everyone focused on him, Robinson locked eyes with Rice. "He looked at me, I looked at him," Rice says, "as if [to say]—this is it. This is time for redemption. And I didn't think Rumeal was going to miss. I don't know what everyone else was thinking, but I was like, 'He's got this. This game is in the bag.'"

Rice was right. Robinson dropped the tying free throw neatly through the hoop and then did the same with the potential game-winner. Robinson had redeemed himself at the best possible moment and put Michigan ahead by one point. "He stepped up there and knocked 'em down like the champion that we said he was," Rice says.

But there were still three seconds on the clock. In the huddle before Robinson's free throws, "Fisher had said, 'Well, when Rumeal makes these two free throws, this is what we're gonna do defensively,'" Mills recalls. "So that was more or less what we prepared for….Because this team is red hot, and we've got to worry about this team getting the ball and making the shot."

Per Fisher's instructions, all five Wolverines dropped back on defense. Seton Hall's Ramos prepared to throw the ball in, but Fisher called a timeout. When Michigan returned to the court, Mills, instead of dropping back, walked forward to the baseline. Ramos would have to throw over the 6-foot-11 center.

Under the circumstances, the pass was well executed, as Walker caught it in the frontcourt with enough time to shoot, albeit from long range. Critically, however, Michigan had kept the ball away from the more dangerous outside gunners, Morton and Gaze; Walker had missed his only 3-point shot that season, and his second try was no better. Walker turned and released his desperation shot, which glanced high off the backboard before Rice caught the ball and clutched it safely as the buzzer sounded.

Michigan 80, Seton Hall 79. The Wolverines were national champions for the first time in the school's history.

"It was like, 'Hallelujah!'" Vaught says. "We had finally accomplished everything that we had talked about, prayed about, practiced hard for and put up with a bunch of stuff for. It was the moment. And that's just when you want to hug your teammates, hug your coaches, look around at all those people and let it all sink in. Because who knows if you'll ever accomplish anything on that level, on that magnitude, ever again. Very few people ever do. So when it's happening, you just want to look around and let it sink in and get into you, so you can always remember that. Streamers falling and people hugging and all that Maize and Blue going nuts."

"Unbelievable," Rice says of the moment of victory. "Finally. Mission accomplished." Rice recalls Robinson "jumping up into my arms, I'm like, 'Man, it's over. We did it. We did it. It's over.' It was such a relief, and we were so excited. That was one of the best feelings in the world at that time. We accomplished what we set out to do." Rice says his thoughts then turned to "all the people that helped us get there. Past players. Past coaches. Bill Frieder.… It was just something that we knew that we were going to treasure forever. Something we all did together, as family and as friends. And to say that it was a first for the University of Michigan, that was one of the proudest moments."

Clearly, the first hero of the moment was Robinson, who finished with 21 points and a championship game record 11 assists. Additionally, his 56 assists remains the second-best one-tournament total, as of 2023.

The star of the entire tournament—and the easy MVP choice—was Rice. The senior finished his incredible NCAA run with 31 points and led U-M with 11 rebounds. His final triple broke Mike McGee's school scoring record, which at the time was also the Big Ten scoring mark. He'd scored 184 points in the six NCAA tournament games, breaking Bill Bradley's mark of 177 set in 1965. Through 2023, Rice's record still stands.

Glen Rice holds up the trophy as the Wolverines celebrate their 1989 NCAA title. *Duane Black.*

"After each game, I didn't let myself get satisfied," Rice says. "I always believed that, OK, the next team we play, they're definitely going to be focused on me. So I have to keep trying to find ways of doing things differently or continue to keep building up my endurance. Because I always felt that was going to be a huge plus for the other side if they find a way to stop me."

THE MAN WHO WASN'T THERE

After beating Seton Hall, Fisher's ascension as the new head coach was assured. But the players didn't forget the old one. Bill Frieder had led the Wolverines up to the Promised Land, but like Moses before him, he hadn't been allowed to enter.

Frieder "recruited everyone to get there," Mills says, "and for him not to be able to enjoy it…that kind of bothers me to this day. Because he was a great man; he got us all there. And I really felt that it was just our time. We would've won it with him or without him. Because him and Fisher had the same philosophy."

Grant calls Frieder "more of a Michigan man than anybody else that was there. He's from that area, he coached all those years backing up Johnny Orr. He's a Michigan man. And for him not to be able to coach, that wasn't right.…It makes it seem that they were right because they ended up winning the whole thing anyway. So it's a no-win situation either way."

"When I couldn't coach the team," Frieder says, "my exact quote was, 'If this is the worst thing that happens to me in my lifetime, I'll have a great life.' And I continued to root for the team. I talked to Fisher almost on a daily basis throughout the tournament.…So I'm pulling for all my might, and I was proud of Steve Fisher with the job he did. So I didn't get to coach the last six games, and we won the national championship and we'll never know what would've happened if I was the coach. But we got it done, and that was very, very satisfying for me, because it was the culmination of a decade of hard work."

In the end, Steve Fisher coached a Bill Frieder–recruited team, using Bill Frieder's system, to the national championship. It was far too late in the season to change Michigan's style decisively, but did any of Fisher's unique touches make the difference that put the Wolverines over the top? As Frieder says, we'll never know. But one thing is certain: Frieder's firing and Fisher's ascension injected emotions into the mix that wouldn't have been there had Frieder continued to coach. And those motivations were clearly a key to Michigan's unique tournament run.

Later, when the school ordered championship rings, Fisher put Frieder's name on the list, but somewhere along the line, his name was removed. Fisher then purchased an additional ring on his own and sent it to Frieder.

A Dream Come True

Reflecting on the championship, Hughes says the triumph "is what we talked about. Glen and I—four years [previously].…Winning the national title for the University of Michigan, with a great group of guys that had one mission."

And it was fitting that Strack, whose teams laid the foundation for the modern Michigan basketball program, was on hand as the school won its first NCAA basketball championship. "I thought that was one of the more exciting basketball games I've ever seen," Strack says. "It was a very exciting time for Michigan basketball."

"Obviously," Rice says, "when you think about the history, you don't wish we were the first ones. But being that we were, it was just that extra pride that you not only had for the team that accomplished it, but finally, the University of Michigan has one under their belt."

Rice went on to enjoy a fifteen-year NBA career and earned another ring as a starter for the Los Angeles Lakers' 2000 NBA championship squad. On February 20, 2005, Rice's no. 41 was the fourth Michigan jersey honored at Crisler Arena.

While in the NBA, Rice says, then-Houston coach Rudy Tomjanovich told him, "'We're all proud of you guys. The whole Michigan alumni, the whole family, all proud of you.' We hear that everywhere we go. And we owe a lot to them, our fans. Because they carried us, too."

BIBLIOGRAPHY

Brief quotes were taken from various issues of the *Ann Arbor News*, *Detroit News*, *Sporting News*, *Sports Illustrated* and *Wolverine* magazine, as well as the Big Ten Network documentary *Greatest Seasons: 1989 Basketball—Michigan*.

Beckett, John. *Mission Accomplished!* South Bend, IN: Diamond Communications Inc., 1989.

Bell, Taylor. *Glory Days: Legends of Illinois High School Basketball*. Champaign, IL: Sports Publishing LLC, 2006.

Canham, Don, with Larry Paladino. *From the Inside*. Ann Arbor, MI: Olympia Sports Press, 1996.

Frieder, Bill, with Jeff Mortimer. *Basket Case*. Chicago: Bonus Books Inc., 1988.

Hemingway, Tom, with Bill Haney. *Life Among the Wolverines*. South Bend, IN: Diamond Communications, 1985.

Madej, Bruce. *Michigan: Champions of the West*. Champaign, IL: Sports Publishing, 1997.

McGovern, Gene. *Here's Johnny Orr*. Ames: Iowa State University Press, 1992.

Mortimer, Jeff. *Pigeons, Bloody Noses and Little Skinny Kids*. Dexter, MI: Thomson-Shore Publishers Inc., 1978.

Russell, Cazzie L., Jr. *Me, Cazzie Russell*. Old Tappan, NJ: Fleming H. Revell Company, 1967.

Schembechler, Bo, and John U. Bacon. *Bo's Lasting Lessons*. New York: Business Plus, 2007.

Tomjanovich, Rudy, with Robert Falkoff. *A Rocket at Heart*. New York: Simon & Schuster, 1997.

University of Michigan National Championship. Charlotte, NC: UMI Publications Inc., 1989.

ABOUT THE AUTHOR

Mike Rosenbaum is a veteran Detroit-area sportswriter and editor who's covered everything from high school and amateur sports to the Super Bowl and the NCAA basketball tournament. His previous book, *Wolverine: A Photographic History of Michigan Football*, was published by the Michigan History Project in 2015. He served as columnist and sports editor with the *Detroit Jewish News* and was a sports editor at the *Observer & Eccentric Newspapers*, where he earned numerous writing and editing awards. He's been published by the *Detroit Free Press*, *USA Today*, the *Lansing State Journal*, the *Royal Oak Tribune* and *Hockey Digest*, among other publications, and wrote the track and field website for About.com. He was also a radio sports reporter for WABX-FM.